EVOCATIVENESS

EVOCATIVENESS

Moving and Persuasive Interventions in Psychotherapy

Stephen A. Appelbaum, Ph.D.

JASON ARONSON INC.
Northvale, New Jersey
London

This book was set in 12 pt. Bembo by Alabama Book Composition of Deatsville, AL, and printed and bound by Book-mart Press, Inc. of North Bergen, NJ.

10   9   8   7   6   5   4   3   2   1

Library of Congress Cataloging-in-Publication Data

Appelbaum, Stephen A.
    Evocativeness : moving and persuasive interventions in psychotherapy /
Stephen A. Appelbaum.
       p.   cm.
    Includes bibliographical references and index.
    ISBN 0–7657–0246–0
      1. Psychotherapy. 2. Psychotherapy—Philosophy. 3. Psychotherapy—Case studies.
4. Evocation. I. Title.

RC480.5 .A673 2000
616.89'14—dc21
                                          00–028853

Printed in the United States of America on acid-free paper. For information and catalog write to Jason Aronson Inc., 230 Livingston Street, Northvale, NJ 07647-1726, or visit our website: www.aronson.com

Contents

Acknowledgments

Dr. Brooks Appelbaum's skills and interests range from the study of nineteenth-century women novelists to theater acting, directing, and playwriting. Nonetheless, she blessedly found time to edit and add to this book.

She was joined in these tasks by my longtime colleague, Dr. Michael Harty, who, busy as he always is, never seems too busy to contribute editorially to my writings. Dr. Jeane Whitehouse gave the manuscript the benefit of her perceptive editorial eye while at the same time supplying much appreciated support and encouragement. (I don't always scrupulously follow editorial advice, and so any lapses may well be my fault.) Jason Aronson, as is usual for him, sparked the work with key ideas.

Much of this book was written at the Austen Riggs Center, Stockbridge, Massachusetts, as part of my responsibility there as the Erik Erikson Scholar in Residence, 1996–1997. That fellowship afforded me a great writing opportunity, which continued while I was Visiting Professor, Department of Psychiatry, Harvard Medical School.

The first statement of the book's thesis appeared in print when I was a staff member of the Menninger Clinic, Topeka, Kansas. But beyond that, my years there have found their way subtly but decisively into all aspects of my professional self. For that shaping of self and career I will always be grateful.

Finally I am indebted indeed to those therapists and patients who allowed their work to be included; they showed rare courage and devotion.

We do not see the actual things themselves; in most cases, we confine ourselves to reading the labels affixed to them . . . Deep in our souls we should hear the strains of our inner life's unbroken melody—a music that is ofttimes gay, but more frequently, plaintive and always original.

—Henri Bergson

To the Reader:

A CALL FOR CASES

The publisher requests that readers who come across examples of successful evocative interventions (or failures) e-mail editor@ aronson.com, or write to Jason Aronson Inc., 230 Livingston Street, Northvale, NJ 07647. Your clinical vignettes will make the next edition of this book a richer and more useful work. Please provide a verbatim account of the interaction between patient and therapist, along with clarifying commentary.

PART I

SOMETHING UNCONTROLLED IS GOING ON HERE

1

Introducing a New Old Friend

Most psychotherapists know a good intervention from a bad one—whether it is moving, persuasive, and memorable, or dull, pedestrian, and inconsequential. They may, however, be much less sure of why it is one way or another and of the best way to make the delivery of their own interventions more effective. In this book we will try to answer such questions. To launch us, here is a brief vignette.

The hospital billing department alerted the therapist that his patient had not paid his psychotherapy bill for the past three months.

T: I understand that you haven't paid your psychotherapy bill for some time.

P: Oh, it's been hard to catch up this summer.

Trying to pay a little here and
a little there (pause) especially
since losing my job. (Pause.)
I've been paying what I can,
but I know I'm behind.

T: It really seems like a dark
cloud hovering over your
head.

P: And I don't know how to
get out of it! The money
that we put aside is dwindling, and I'm beginning to
think that it won't be easy
to get another position. (1)

(1) The therapist's "dark cloud"
image evocatively speaks
the language of depression.
"Hanging over your head"
speaks the language of anticipa-
tory anxiety, perhaps bordering
on panic ("I don't know how to
get out of it"). The therapist's
resonance at that moment seems
to have encouraged the patient
toward enlarging the meaning
to him of his predicament, for
the patient adds a dwindling
theme. His choice of "dwindling" suggests that he equates
his financial impotence with

sexual impotence. The ongoing gerund form suggests that he feels that his dwindling is steadily getting worse. He begins to worry about a complete collapse, an inability to find a solution ("another position"). The therapist should be able to continue the resonance thus established with the patient with some such remark as, "You seem not only to feel sad and regretful, but deeply worried. Perhaps your difficulty paying your bill right now lights up a lifelong worry about being the man you would like to be— capable, a problem-solver, potent."

This brief passage pithily illustrates how an evocative empathic remark can encourage elaboration, derivatives, and the patient's own evocativeness. Instead of referring to the ominous "dark cloud" feeling, the therapist could have gone further in the bill-collecting mode, or focused on the patient's "guilt" and "depression" using those overused clinical words, or countless other interventions,

> ranging from dull to disastrous.
> Instead, the therapist and the
> patient took steps toward a
> cloudless sky.

There are sunsets, and there are sunsets. Some dusks, the sun just quietly slips away. Other dusks, one stares at the changing sky transfixed, or runs for a camera. We are surrounded by such variations in color, drama, and impact. And like fish who seem unaware of the water because of its omnipresence, we tend to overlook the varying degrees by which our surroundings capture our imaginations and move us.

I call these variations in emotional and sensory impact "evocativeness." If there were such a thing as a meter to measure evocativeness, we could put the meter on anything and get a reading, an indication of the thing's capacity to evoke a response. Sometimes the capacity is inherent, as in a purple orchid, a redolent stew, the luminous light of an eye. Sometimes evocativeness is enlisted. This is true for the arts, and for the artistic, creative aspect of psychotherapy. A high reading on the evocativeness meter, for a speech in the theater as for the delivery of an interpretation, indicates the difference between an unevocative, gray, forgettable blip on one's sensory screen and a profound experience that embodies nuances of the present, reminders of the past, and intimations of the future. That movement on the evocative meter reflects the amazing amalgam of feeling and thought that *communicates* rather than just communicates.

For a fanciful, heuristic example, take what would happen if I were to read aloud to you a few pages of the phone book. Almost surely you would either fall asleep, or excuse yourself to get to a suddenly remembered appointment. If, say, Al Pacino or Meryl

Streep were to read aloud the same pages, chances are much better that you would stick around.

Or picture yourself, at the end of a play or movie, making the journey from your seat out to the lobby, then into the outside world. After some theater performances or films, you will have forgotten the experience by the time you hit the sidewalk. After others you revel in the pity and terror of it all, are haunted by reminders the next few days and nights, and may remember and learn from that memory for the rest of your life.

Remarkably, a fictional story in an artificial medium makes a new existence seem alive—in a way parallel to what happens, in the circumscribed setting of a psychotherapy session and with a real story, when a new vision of life emerges. In the world of theater, both the memorable and forgettable may have been lovingly crafted by world-class artists supported by millions of dollars. Both came into being by way of predictions of success made by skilled producers, directors, actors, and writers. Yet one of the productions soars across the artistic firmament while the other vanishes ignominiously. The reasons for one or another outcome are unknown or minimized at the beginning, and often not fully understandable at the end. *Something uncontrolled is going on here.*

Just as certain works of art move us and others do not, the same is true with regard to psychotherapeutic sessions. In some sessions, feelings and ideas are so powerfully communicated and experienced that not only does the patient cry or exult, but so (usually inwardly) does the therapist. In other sessions, both therapist and patient may find themselves privately ruminating over where to go for lunch. There are therapists who inspire, create, and evoke, and there are therapists who leave the listener cold, uninvolved, and bored. Some people progress in psychotherapy who, by various familiar criteria, should never be able to, while others, slated for success, fail to progress to the degree that one had every technical right to expect. Therapists with the same training, knowledge, and apparent skill may get vastly different results. *Something uncontrolled is going on here.*

I suggest that what is going on here, in therapy as in art, is the therapeutic wild card that I call *evocativeness.*

According to the dictionary, evocativeness means "calling out; summoning forth, as from seclusion or from the grave." Its etymological root is *vox* or voice. Other dictionary meanings especially relevant to psychotherapy are "tending by artistic imaginative means to re-create (a mood, time, place, or personality)" and "tending to inspire or evoke vivid memories, recollections, or associations." Aristotle (McKeon 1941) could have been referring to evocativeness when he wrote, "The business of every art is to bring something into existence."

In psychotherapy, the first voice refers to the transmission of meaning as gleaned by the "third ear." In psychotherapy the third ear, as taken from Theodore Reik's famous book title *Listening with the Third Ear,* refers to the ferreting out of latent content, the fruit of psychological-mindedness, to insight. The "first voice," then, refers to manifest content, the basic bare bones of the messages. However it is gathered, the therapy task is to transmit information by way of the "second voice." In so doing when we speak with the second voice, that meaning becomes significant as patient and therapist enter a new realm of vividness, intimacy, and understanding. Psychotherapists have emphasized the first voice and the "third ear" to an extent that has at best minimized and at worst overlooked the "second voice."

The emphasis on "the third ear"—understanding and interpreting—was an accident of history. Freud's interest, as it had to be at the time and under the circumstances of discovery, was in developing a theory. He pursued that interest first through hypnosis, then by summoning thoughts through placing his hands on the foreheads of patients. Dissatisfied with the yield from these procedures, he enlisted free associations, especially to dreams, to bring into awareness clues and solutions to the mystery, answers to the ultimate motivational question, "Why?" In those earliest days psychoanalysis was conceived of as a simplistic information theory. By decoding messages from the sender, Freud as the receiver learned the "sense" of what had hitherto been a jumble.

Freud's clues were based on the recognition that language both denotes and connotes. When it denotes, it means exactly what it says, no more no less. When it connotes, language means what it says, only more so. Words offer clues to levels of meaning within, beneath, and beyond meanings; they direct one to what are sometimes wisps, sometimes waves, of feelings, and create sensations that readers or listeners may only later comprehend, or, even without comprehending, respond to. Truth is only possible when it includes passion; passion is only fully possible when it includes truth. So in the interstices between facts and feelings, denotations and connotations, lie textures of experience. In the mysterious space between words and feelings lurk echoes, surprises, and seductions into ordinarily hidden ego states, selves, fears, and hopes—all that makes humans human. Success in bringing the hidden significance of words to useful emotional awareness depends on one's capacity for evocativeness. One listens with the third ear to learn about the range and detail of experience, one speaks with the first voice to convey the fundamental meaning, and one uses the second voice of evocativeness to make experience live.

It would be tempting and easy to designate as facts those aspects that the third ear is designed to ferret out, and to call what the second voice evokes feelings. But that would damage psychological reality. We separate intellect and feeling for heuristic and other practical reasons, but the data of psychotherapy are unitary, just as body and mind are. One can know a fact if the purpose of the knowing is factual; one can know a feeling if the purpose of knowing is to have or recognize an emotion. But the knowing of psychotherapeutic data is neither solely factual nor solely emotional. Every mental content, idea, or feeling has its substrate in drive, as Rapaport (1950) demonstrated through his precise system. The therapist, in practice, does not simply teach an idea, nor does the therapist simply encourage a feeling, nor does the therapist even simply enable a patient to enliven an idea with feeling or control a feeling with an idea. What the therapist does, in addition, is to help the patient to have—through transference or by way of recall— experiences in the present that are ordinarily unavailable.

Richfield (1954) bridges the conventional divide between fact and emotion when—quoting Bertrand Russell—he distinguishes between knowledge by description and knowledge by acquaintance. Knowledge by acquaintance is the way most people know the effects of alcohol—that is, experientially; knowledge by description is the way most people know the effects of strychnine— only by way of having some facts about it, or indirectly, as by analogy or inference. In order for a patient to integrate feeling and fact, and to experience emotional healing, she must replace remote or unacknowledged impressions (knowledge by description) with the immediate and experiential (knowledge by acquaintance). Proceeding from Freud's aphorism, that one cannot overcome an enemy who is absent, Richfield writes:

> When our insights are knowledge by description, we have truths about the repressed enemy, not the enemy itself. The latter is known directly only when brought through the psychological barriers of the mind. Our insight is then knowledge by acquaintance. . . . Only when knowledge takes this form is it possible for the cognitive object to receive the necessary integration into the

ego. The conscious personality cannot learn to handle a need of which it is unaware. But the awareness must have the need itself as its object, and not merely facts about it before changes in the distribution of cathexes are to be brought about.

Kris (1952) puts it this way: the full investment by the ego, the syntonicity of the event with superego and id striving, may then lead to the feeling of certainty, and to the change from "I know of" to "I believe." Eissler (1965) offers two criteria of knowledge from the psychoanalytic point of view. First, it

> must not be isolated from the subject's previous knowledge, but must be in maximum associative connection with all systems of the personality . . . all of the implications inherent in an intellectual context must come to the subject's awareness. Second, knowledge . . . is evaluated primarily in terms of the emotional reverberations of the particular content. *Indifference to knowledge is tantamount to the absence of knowledge.* [author's italics]

The poet Paul Valéry, as quoted by Herbert Read (1950), captures this union of emotion and intellect:

> What is sung or articulated in the most solemn and the most critical moments of life; what we hear in a Liturgy; what is murmured or groaned in the extremity of passion; what claims a child or the afflicted; what attests the truth of an oath—these are words of a particular tone and expression which cannot be resolved into clear ideas, nor separated out, without making them absurd or silly. In all these cases, the accent and inflection of the voice outweigh anything intelligible conveyed to us: it is our life rather than our mind which is addressed—I would say that such words incite us to *become* rather than excite us to *understand*.

Note the venerable age of many of these references. Remarkably, despite the advances made by modern theorists, and especially by relational theorists in conceptualizing and exploiting affects and subjectivity, these issues and challenges still vex us. In art, science, and psychotherapy, we continue to struggle to be fully human.

I would not be surprised if my going back and forth between psychotherapy and art didn't raise some eyebrows. Physicians, brought up from the ranks of those trained in technology, and psychologists, who have to hurdle the requirements of science, are rarely encouraged to think of psychotherapy as an art and to scrutinize the relationship of art to science. If we look more closely at evocativeness, however, we find some surprising kinships.

The therapist's scientific task is to decode the patient's associations, unravel the symbolism, clarify, reduce, connect, and—for purposes of theory—define terms with precision and as operationally as possible. This was Freud's mission when he was constructing his theories and trying to suppress the artist in himself. By contrast, the artist evokes through connotation rather than denotation. Art proceeds by indirection, from hints to symbolism. It is mysterious. The novelist Willa Cather (1995) put it this way:

> Whatever is felt upon the page without being specifically named there—that, one might say is created. It is the inexplicable presence of the thing not named, of the overtone divined by the ear but not heard by it, the verbal mood, the emotional aura of the fact or the thing or the deed, that gives high quality to the novel or the drama, as well as to poetry itself.

Mallarmé says simply, "To name something is to destroy three-quarters of the pleasure of poetry." The goal of the artist is to "evoke something little by little, in order to show a state of the soul." Along with his scientific task, the therapist has a similar artistic one. At those moments, despite our traditional emphasis on the scientific aspect of psychotherapy, the artist's goal and the goal of psychotherapy are one and the same. Let us examine this similarity further.

In order to show a state of the soul, there must be a soul and there must be someone to show it to. Conventionally, in art, the soul is the artist, and the listener or viewer is the audience. However, some aestheticians have seen these as shared roles, and others have noted that the audience is the creator: the way a work of art is experienced depends on the ability of the audience to register and to appreciate what is inherent in the work.

One way to view communication in psychotherapy is to see the patient and the therapist as each taking on, at different times, the roles of both audience and artist. The therapist plays the role of audience when he listens with the third ear, proving the mystery of motivations and intentions. He creates new meaning out of the patient's words by accepting these words in a receptive and creative way. In this phase of the exchange, the (artist) patient struggles to bring to the audience's (therapist's) awareness the ordinarily hidden meanings. As David Beres (1957) puts it, "What is communicated is a creation of the analysand, who becomes in a sense a creative artist." Unwitting as patients may be of their craft, they employ symbolism, condensation, metaphor, displacement, and sometimes the grammar of the primary process to communicate their message. They may have no conscious interest at all in doing this aesthetically, but, driven by the wish to express, and goaded by feelings struggling for expression, they sense that the more aesthetic their production, the more likely it is to be heard, understood, remembered, and acted upon. With regard to maximally evocative occasions, a therapist—perhaps surprised by the patient's unwonted felicity of expression—will remark with awe how moved or entranced the patient made him feel. The patient is like the artist who, for long stretches in his day-to-day life, and even in his artistic endeavors, fails to be evocative, but then (inexplicably, it seems) hits the heights.

At another point in the psychotherapeutic exchange, the therapist becomes the artist. He takes the clues, hints, adumbrations scattered here and there by the patient, and begins the process of interpretation. The patient—who has been making do with his own half-understanding, or perhaps his confused, defensive, and distorted versions—becomes the audience. It is now up to the therapist to be sufficiently the artist to meet the challenge of evocativeness. The therapist has to confirm what Lionel Trilling (1955) said about Freud's view of the mind: that it is a poetry-making faculty. Beres (1957) writes:

> [The therapist] collaborates in the creative process by supplying the skill of the poet to bring to the surface emotions and images (which are id derivatives) but to keep them controlled within the demands of the ego. . . . The analyst's role is not simply to translate to the patient the meanings of the derivatives of the unconscious. Rather the role of the analyst is to free the patient's imagination so that he may re-create the fantasies of his childhood and communicate them to himself and to the analyst. . . . The patient then re-experiences his emotions, recollects, reconstructs and relives; and in this accomplishes the conviction that marks the true insight of the analytic experience which provides "the willing suspension of disbelief" that leads to the sense of conviction.

Strachey (1934) makes the same point in stating his case for the effectiveness of the immediacy of transference interpretation: "every mutative interpretation must be emotionally 'immediate'; the patient must experience it as something actual . . . of a certain intensity."

For what it may be worth to another's sensibilities, when I am conscious of the task of therapeutic evocativeness, I feel much as I do when I write poetry or improvise jazz on my saxophone. I recognize the task and realize that I can either somewhat automatically churn something out or I can dig deep and move to the consciousness of nothing at all to hold onto, into a creative moment when one leaves the humdrum and the well-worn and enters, but not yet safely, the limitless possibilities, the challenge, the demand, the seduction, the welling up that requires release and provides avenues for release. Sometimes literally, sometimes figuratively, I take a deep breath and let the ideas come to mind, then actively select the words and delivery that I want. In other words I "regress in the service of the ego." Sometimes the process is as studied as that, and sometimes it happens more quickly and seemingly more intuitively. Upon a moment's reflection I know when I do it, and pretty much whether I got it right. Exactly the same goes for psychotherapeutic interventions.

To the therapist (artist) this act of freeing the patient's imagination with answering words and interpretive images can feel like Plato's ancient model of inspiration:

> and as the Corybantian revelers when they dance are not in their right mind, so the lyric poets are not in their right mind when they are composing their beautiful strains; but when falling under the power of music and metre they are inspired and possessed; like Bacchic maidens who draw milk and honey from the rivers when they are under the influence of Dionysus but not when they are in their right mind.

More recently, Gestalt therapists put this vision of inspiration tartly as, "Get sane—go out of your mind." Introspections by artists of all kinds reveal a sense that the art paints itself, the poem writes itself, the music plays itself—and so some psychotherapists report that when they are "on" they do not know what they are going to say until they have said it. About the writing of *Death of a Salesman*, Arthur Miller (Lahr 1999) called himself "a stenographer. It sort of unveiled itself." Elia Kazan (Lahr 1999) said Miller didn't write *Death of a Salesman*, he released it.

These depictions of creative moments are compelling and undoubtedly accurate—at least for some of us, some of the time. Because my purpose is to argue that at least up to a point evocativeness can be learned, however, these accounts should not be read as indicators of talent or genius—the sort one is either born with or without. Nor should these heady accounts be viewed as an invitation to license or a celebration of the basically undisciplined mind. Such readings neglect the fact that artists and evocative psychotherapists are *trained*. Their apparent epiphanies issue from prepared backgrounds.

Here is a little story about learning to be evocative that Merton Gill told about himself:

> When I was a junior staff member at the Menninger Clinic, in the early 40's, my turn came to present at one of our regular staff meetings . . . when I finished, the late Karl Menninger, who ran those meetings, declared with an acerbity that was not entirely uncharacteristic of him, "Merton, I have never known anyone else with your capacity to make something intrinsically so lively and exciting so dull and boring." Of course he was right, and I have been struggling against that propensity ever since.

And what propensity was Gill struggling against? Presumably it was the same one that Hamlet protests against: "You would seem to know my steps and you would pluck out the heart of my mystery; you would sound me from the lowest note to the top of my compass and there is excellent service in this little organ; yet cannot you make it speak" (III, ii). As we all do from time to time, Gill and Hamlet were struggling against the fear that lies below the surface, one or another vicissitude of the impulse life. Those who deal with evocativeness are especially vulnerable to that fear. Dithering on the surface—resisting—is often the boring outcome.

When I talk about "surface," I am using Freud's archaeological metaphor, his expression of the depth dimension. In recent years, relational therapists have objected to this image as indicating a one-person psychology that emphasizes the work of probing the unconscious to the exclusion of much else. Yet the task of evocation *is* to push from surface to depth, to move from quotidian words to words with depth reverberations, to images, then finally simply to feeling. In recognizing that the therapeutic task importantly includes moving from words to images, one is using the dimension of depth, both with regard to digging back in time and digging down to the unconscious. One does not analyze up, one analyzes down. One burrows into and down for the layers of meaning embedded in words, as Thass-Theinemann (1963) has pointed out.

The very word "evoke" suggests depth, having its linguistic inception in the image of summoning forth, "as from seclusion or the grave." So long as one subscribes to the fundamental idea of images coming before words—the preverbal life—one is committed to remembering as far back (as deeply) as possible, and taking seriously the communication in dreams (as well as art) that is dependent upon buried imagery. In a telling experiment, Renneker and colleagues (1960) listened repeatedly to therapy transcripts, and found that each new hearing revealed more and more to the group of therapist-researchers. They likened the experience to looking through a microscope, each increase in power revealing more of the teeming life not otherwise discernible. As A. E.

Housman (1933) put it, "And I think that to transfuse emotions—
not to transmit thought but to set up in the reader's sense a
vibration corresponding to what was felt by the writer—is the
peculiar function of poetry." As applied to therapy, the therapist
(reader) experiences in himself what he senses is vibrating or
resonating in the patient (writer). What that is may be apparent on
the surface, though it more usually requires depth exploration, an
exploration that the two vibrating, resonating participants do
together. And so the one-person/two-person controversy collapses
in the face of the intimate two-person work-relationships that
evocatively result in making the unconscious conscious.

Thus far, I have spoken of evocativeness largely in terms of
words. That is not surprising, since words are the main avenue of
communication in the "talking therapies." In his "Introductory
Lectures," Freud writes,

> Words were originally magic and to this day words have retained
> much of their ancient magical power. By words one person can
> make another blissfully happy or drive him to despair, by words the
> teacher conveys his knowledge to his pupils, by words the orator
> carries his audience with him and determines their judgments and
> decisions. Words provoke affects and are in general the means of
> mutual influence among men. Thus we shall not depreciate the use
> of words in psychotherapy and we shall be pleased if we can listen to
> the words that pass between the analyst and his patient.

In "The Question of Lay Analysis" he (1926) writes,

> and incidentally do not let us despise the *word*. After all it is a
> powerful instrument; it is the means by which we convey our
> feelings to one another, our method of influencing other people.
> Words can do unspeakable good and cause terrible wounds. No

doubt in the beginning was the deed and the word came later; in some circumstances it meant an advance in civilization when deeds were softened into words. But originally the word was magic—a magical act; and it has retained much of its ancient power.

It should be understood, however, that the same principles of evocativeness apply to the nonverbal expressive pursuits: fine art, sculpture, dance. These arts, too, can be ranked in terms of evocativeness and they can be enhanced by awareness of its challenge and by the employment of those devices that can influence it.

2

The Eternal Duality

E vocativeness takes its place within the long struggle in Western philosophy to integrate thought and feeling. This struggle has its substrate in the physiology and anatomy of the brain: the ancient, original primitive brain buried deep in the head, and the more recently developed cerebral lobes. The ancient brain continues its losing battle to maintain the viability of the senses of smell and touch even as, under the Darwinian lash, the new brain increasingly exploits sight and hearing. The ancient brain, with its intimate connection with the viscera, reverberates with passion and discharges tension through action. The new brain attempts to delay action in time to apply reason, to anticipate consequences, and to synchronize the demands of contemporary, external reality with the peremptory impulses of the human animal.

Humans start life as primitive beings mainly invested in the body, having what Freud called "body ego." That view was affirmed by Ferenczi (1913): "Language arises out of original feeling-forms. It begins with the body." The next step, still preverbal, seems to be a sensitivity to variations in sounds. In the depth of the mind, where vibrations and resonances constitute the language, words may be less important than intonation. The child understands the moods and spirit of his mother long before he understands words. Even severely deteriorated, language-regressed and wordless aphasic patients are able to perceive and discriminate intonation patterns. The baby's babbling, while in the ultimate service of learning to form words, serves as communication by way of changes in volume and intonation. In trying to answer his self-imposed question—"How to establish an emotionally meaningful dialogue without using words?"—Killingmo (1995) concludes there are instances when "Only the very tone of the voice can break through to experiential states beyond semantics." A classic device for training actors is to challenge them to create an emotionally charged dialogue with a partner using only gibberish—and thereby to "break through," to use Killingmo's phrase, their traditional dependence on language. Steiner (1987) notes that evocative intonation "brings to life internal and external objects on the psychic stage of our inner world . . . there is no doubt that intonation does play a fundamental role in analysis, because it is linked with extremely primitive, nearly *osmotic* interchange of feelings."

Despite his devotion to the study of the body and its place in his emerging psychology, Freud saw the interpersonal importance of the baby's cry as early as his 1895 paper, "Project for a Scientific Psychology." There he suggested that the fact that the mother understands the cry (which we can tell by her correct response to it) spurs the development of verbal language. Encouraged by nonverbal communication, the baby sets off on the perilous path into the verbal land of nonsense and sense, the grammars of primary and secondary processes.

As usual, there is a range of possible outcomes to this journey. Taking the extreme, there are those who largely cut themselves off from the impulse life and the opportunities that impulse life provides for evocativeness. Yet they go through the motions of life unexceptionally. They are normal to the nth degree: supernormal. Of these supernormal, Winnicott writes, "there are those who are so firmly anchored in objectively perceived reality that they are . . . out of touch with the subjective world and with the creative approach to fact." Bollas (1987) writes of "a particular drive to be normal, one that is typified by the numbing and eventual erasure of subjectivity in favor of a self that is conceived as a material object among other man-made products in the object world." He writes also of a "normative illness . . . typified by a radical break with subjectivity and by profound absence of the subjective element in everyday life." People who have so thoroughly muted their passions present enormous challenges for the therapist. Havens writes: "The whole psychoanalytic assumption of a treatment relationship that can mobilize the patient's deepest attachments and thus change them by the examination of these attachments (what Freud called 'the cure through love') collapses in the presence of such tepid, disinterested people." Such powerful, determining inhibitions can come by way of an hysteriform route based on repression, or by way of an obsessive-compulsive route based on isolation of affect, or a schizoid route based on detachment from others.

What Winnicott calls the super*abnormals*, by contrast, are unable to use language to anticipate consequences, control behaviors, and communicate meaningfully with others. Thus, they tend to be action-oriented and are as likely as not to pose behavior problems. Hyperinvolved in vigorous interaction with the environment, they eschew the inward, regressive moves toward the affective pool from which evocativeness can be drawn.

This somewhat Manichean duality plays itself out in the dialectic, the tension, that runs through all human affairs, the major aspects of which are often labeled *romanticism* and *classicism* (Appelbaum 1990). In general terms, these polarities are expressed as form and substance, age and youth, formal and informal; the first of each of these dualities represents the classical position. In psychiatry and psychology the polarities show themselves in the dimension of obsessive-compulsive and hysterical personalities. The (classical) obsessive-compulsive emphasizes thought before action, worries over cleanliness and accuracy, invokes abstract principles to explain and guide decisions, and puts great stock in being right, among other traits. By contrast, the (romantic) hysterical personality is characterized by intuition, concreteness, feeling, impulsiveness, and impressionistic thinking.

Hysterical people tend to feel good, or at least to maintain that they do, so it is relatively rare to hear of their dissatisfactions with their natures. It is difficult to imagine the hysterical personality crying out for more order, consistency, and abstraction (and less feeling and intuition). By contrast, the tragically inclined classical personality types typically experience and express frustration about feeling closed off from what they perceive to be a rich, unattainable emotional life; they yearn, in speech and in writing, for release and joy. Considering the educational hurdles that psychotherapists must surmount, it is no surprise that they develop—quite purposefully—at least some degree of classical compulsiveness. Along with this focus on objectivity, however, comes lamentation, ruefulness, and rumination with regard to the tantalizing beyond-the-fingertips affective life.

Even—or perhaps, especially—artists, whom we admire for their expressive facility, recognize this gap between ideas and feelings. Maisel (1994) writes that according to Tolstoy, "In artistic experiences there is a sense of recognition that something has been understood and felt which one already knew, but had been unable to experience." George Santayana (Rose 1987) acknowledges that "The understanding, when not suffused with some glow of sympathetic emotions . . . gives but a dry, crude image of the world." And William Faulkner (1932) longs for an emotional directness that even words cannot achieve: "But words are my talent. I must try to express clumsily in words what the pure music would have done better." Finally, Freud: "The intellectual content of our explanations cannot do it for the patient."

As we travel the difficult path from primitive to sophisticated expression, the best outcome is to be able to choose our own behavior, depending on what circumstances require. Ideally, we learn to adopt, quite genuinely, the consciousness of the accountant, or the poet, or anything in between. The source of evocativeness in the primary process, in the impulse life, is available as needed. In the best "good enough" or best of mother–child relationships, we learn this from mother's flexible response to our infant communication. If our mother fails to respond evocatively and effectively to our needs, we learn that the expression of feelings leads to disappointment and discouragement. Then, as adults, we avoid more disappointment—even shame—by shying away from affect-driven memories, emotional experiences, and artistically engrossing insights. Coldness sets in; indeed, it is welcomed. Only later, perhaps, when the consequences of emotional sterility become apparent, does such a person question that coldness, which— because it impedes evocativeness—has become a deadly enemy. Psychotherapy offers a second chance to experiment with the impulse life in the course of exploring the whole self.

Words are, of course, the basic mode of exchange in psychotherapy, but where evocative communication is concerned, words are not just words. Their effectiveness in contributing to the task of evocativeness is determined by their delivery and choice. Evocative delivery can be influenced by the longish silences between words, brief pauses, clearing of the throat, judicious use of non-words such as "hmm," tone of voice, and rhythm of speech. The choice of words is even more influential. A colorless voice probably detracts less from evocativeness than a colorless choice of words. The evocative therapist uses words like "desolate," "outcast," "treachery," "singing," "verve," and "plunder"—which are multilayered and imagistic—and fewer words like "rejection," "treatment," "dependent," "insecurity," and "passive," which, while once reasonably evocative, have become trivial and tired. The most evocative words deal with mystery on the way to clarity. They hint at and try out ideas and solutions; they build up the steam of credibility. (As they say, when commenting on improvised jazz, "It's got to *build*.") Through evocative experimentation, the therapist and the patient together earn—as artists say—the authoritative interpretation, the revelation that feels like truth. The poet William Carlos Williams, as quoted by Maisel (1992), offers his personal summing up of this process and in so doing speaks for many evocative therapists: "My vocabulary was chosen out of the intensity of my concern."

Words are not the only elements of the therapist–patient collaboration that can render the therapy more or less evocative. To use the analogy of art once more, the evocativeness of a film or play depends, beyond the scripted words, on the actors and the director, on costumes, makeup, settings, the theater space itself, and the advertising and promotion of the production, including the price of the tickets and the means of obtaining them. So, too, the elements of psychotherapy include the clothing and demeanor of the therapist; the address and furnishing of the office; the expectations shared—or not—between therapist and patient; how the two have gotten together; the therapist's reputation, and the match between therapist and patient in terms of sex, age, sibling position, personality traits, and style.

Whether the communications of therapy will be evocative, meaningful, and memorable depends also on the patient's receptivity. Patients vary greatly in their ability to hear and respond to evocativeness. To take a limiting example, some people can even respond to a computer programmed to behave like a therapist. In fact I had such an experience. Although obviously aware that I was "talking" with a machine I did have some sense of being with a person. On the other hand, some people cannot have that sense of being with another person even when actually with a human and evocative therapist.

So evocation requires not only a sender, but a receiver. In the computer example, I achieved something like attunement or empathy with the electronics by way of responding with my inner interpersonal world, my repertoire of historical events, and the availability and experience of objects. A real, human, and evocative therapist similarly stimulates such latent dispositions. I think what Freud meant when he said that narcissistic (psychotic) people could not be analyzed was that such people could not be stimulated by the therapist to summon a sufficient sense of being firmly and consistently with another, so as to make at least a semblance of transference neurosis possible. Such people may be all too susceptible to evocativeness but in a fragmentary and often distorted way. One could say that the whole world is evocative to them. But what is evoked in them is more their own unregulated fantasies and mercurial feelings than a stable, coherent, coordinated message and connection.

As we have seen, the patient and therapist take turns being the audience and the artist. This is also true—and importantly so—in the work of psychotherapy supervision. The supervisee's role is analogous to that of the patient in the sense that the supervisee, like the patient, is learning to become a more evocative and effective communicator. Patients and students naturally vary in their evocativeness; in general, however, the more they can create images evocatively, the more therapists and supervisors can get the nuances of messages and be inspired to communicate evocatively in return.

3

Struggles with the Desired

The assertion that one can learn to become more evocative as a therapist is central to this book. However, before we get deeply into the questions raised by that challenge, we must first explore those resistances and prejudices that help keep us from being more evocative.

First there is the nature of the beast. Evocativeness has an air of mystery around it that parallels that surrounding art. Even Freud, although with excess modesty, declared he was no better able to grapple with art than with women. This mystery is really the mystery of creativity. Much is said about creativity, much use is made of it, but it seems to have an ineffable core that defies ultimate clarity and definitiveness. There is even lack of agreement as to what constitutes art (and evocativeness). Art critics (and psychotherapy supervisors) regularly disagree in their judgments of this somewhat ephemeral quality. What may be evocative to one person may be pedestrian to another and "wild analysis" to someone else. Such lack of agreement, along with shifting fashions and individual differences, impedes wholehearted, spirited exploitation of evocativeness. But we carry on nonetheless. Artworks do not find their way into museums by mere chance. We make do with coalescence.

The very power of evocativeness and art poses a danger to its acceptance. When one confronts remarkable talent, one may admire and enjoy it or become paralyzingly envious of it. Bravura displays of ability that seem to come from out of nowhere are especially galling and humbling. Even the best of us are subject to such experiences. "How come?" we ask. "Why not me?"

Suppose we take that question seriously rather than as merely a rhetorical complaint. The answer to it could easily be that talent stems from inborn constitutional influences. Such influences have in recent years taken a beating as a corrective response to their longtime use as a handy, face-saving cover for ignorance and lack of viable alternatives. Yet research increasingly focuses on individual differences and differentiations present at birth and even before. How other than through taking into account inborn influences could one explain, say, Mozart playing the piano and composing at age 3, or child prodigies of many other kinds?

Chomsky (1971) suggests that our very capacity to understand sentences is rooted in genetic structures of the mind. Modell (1973), too, notes that "the 'facts' of psychoanalysis are perceptually and biologically rooted." He suggests that "The capacity to know the affective state of another human being is a biological given: This capacity is evolutionary, protecting the species by enabling us to communicate through the medium of tone and inflection before we developed verbal language." This ability survives in the capacity for evocativeness.

Unfortunately, seeing evocativeness as constitutional may also exacerbate nihilistic, despairing feelings. We are confronted with limitations in our chosen profession that seem immutable and beyond our control. At the least it hurts our feelings. Something must be done and that something often enough and sadly enough is to turn our backs on the whole issue.

The clinician in us no doubt objects to consigning excessive influence to constitution. How about sublimation, identifications, counteridentifications, and compromise-formations?

Dynamic explanations, of course, abound. Where do they end and constitution and inheritance begin? As it usually does with dialectical dilemmas, the truth is likely to be found in the harmony of synthesis. Freud's complementary series argument shows us that behavior is a mixture of inborn and environmental influences. So our despair is unwarranted. Constitutional factors do dictate limitations—we may have to resign ourselves to the fact that we never will be the equal of Beethoven or Itzhak Perlman. Or, as Artie Shaw, band leader, clarinetist, and author said (with characteristic overstatement) every discipline has just two great ones, Einstein and Newton for physics, and, of course, Benny Goodman and Artie Shaw for clarinet-playing (personal communication).

But so what? There are lots of journeymen violinists doing good work, making contributions, and fulfilling themselves. While constitutional factors set limitations, they do not account for the whole. Instead of turning our backs on the possibilities, we can work with the dynamic influences, those that are rooted in environmental factors and so are in principle analyzable and changeable. The trick is to get to be as good as it is fated for one to be.

Western culture offers us another source of resistance to evocativeness. In the West, evocativeness is identified with the tender-hearted, the romantic, the artistic, and, in our stereotyped view, the feminine. Thus evocativeness is heir to the ambivalence typically associated with these dimensions of life. Many of us are most comfortable identifying with the Marlboro man (to the point that people endanger their health and the health of others in the pursuit of that identity).

Finally, since evocativeness has its roots in the primitive brain's primitive passions, it opposes the cerebral, civilizing, controlling, and in many ways depriving trends. The siren call of the depths can frighten as it tempts us. Raw pleasure is forbidden; when we sense its emergence into awareness it may be felt not only as bad and punishable, but often as a harbinger of madness. As Maisel (1994) quotes Aristotle as saying, "There is no genius without a mixture of madness." Similarly, in *A Midsummer Night's Dream*, Shakespeare illuminates the dark fear that lurks in the wellspring of feeling:

> Lovers and madmen have such seething brains,
> Such shaping phantasies, that apprehend
> More than cool reason ever comprehends.
> The lunatic, the lover, and the poet,
> Are of imagination all compact . . . [Act V, scene i]

These passions must be exhumed and examined if one seeks to become evocative, even though in their violence they warn us against themselves.

One can make a strong case that this folklore link between madness and creativity contributes to the way we shy away from evocativeness. As we have seen, regression in the service of the ego requires the ability to progress as well as the courage to regress. Without a well-functioning ego "regression in the service of the ego" is just regression. Pain lives in the maelstrom of the id; it is inherent when things fail to make immediate sense, when impulse strivings are regularly frustrated, when the ordinary world—controlled, organized, and zealously attached to its hard-won victories over the id—is ever ready to pounce with disapproval, punishment, and added attempts at frustration.

The genius, operating uniquely in the id, does run a risk. For the blessed ones it is a risk worth taking. According to Salman Rushdie (1999), "A writer's injuries are his strengths, and from his wounds will flow his sweetest, most startling dreams."

As we have noted, one way to escape the pain, or threat of pain, is not to regress, but to remain steadfastly on the surface, to flee passion and depth, and to be resolutely normal no matter the cost. In this Faustian bargain, in return for something like safety, the person exchanges creativity, feeling, flexibility, curiosity, and all manner of intrapsychic adventure. The intrepid person, by contrast, accepts and is shaped by pain and the threat of pain.

This formulation applies equally to artists and therapists. Regression more or less in the service of the ego is their stock in trade as they ply their professions and contend with their lives. That capacity to accept and bear pain facilitates immersion by way of empathy with the struggles of their audience—patients, and so contributes to evocativeness. "Madness" has been put at our disposal. But it does take courage.

In the face of all the aforementioned conditions, it is no wonder that the idea of evocativeness has had relatively little influence in the sciences, even those like psychotherapy that would seem to depend upon it. The concept of evocativeness itself—extended, researched, delineated and applied—was available decades ago in the work of Butler (Butler and Rice 1963) and others. They classified therapists' productions according to categories they called Freshness of Words and Combinations, Voice Quality, and Functional Level of Response. With reference to words, Butler writes, "the most highly connotative language possible seems to be poetic, metaphorical language in which much sensory imagery is used . . . the use of metaphor . . . adds vividness and color to the primary evidence." Regarding Voice Quality, these authors ask of the therapist:

Is [the therapist] actually bringing something as a person, something
that provides or generates new interpersonal experience for the
client? Is he simply "present and accounted for"? Or is he actually
removing something from the situation through dullness, weakness,
or through empty and forced attempts to be something which at
that moment he isn't?

Butler and Rice define their Functional Level of Response by
posing the question: "How much are the therapist's remarks
directed at the meaning or impact of experience?" Their classifica-
tion is in some respects an extension of Sharpe's (1950) observation
that the language of clinical psychoanalysis is closer to poetry than
science.

The work of Butler and others never made it outside the world
of psychology, and with the diminished interest in the work of Carl
Rogers, with which it was associated, it is no longer much attended
to in psychology either. My own experience is perhaps also instruc-
tive. I published an article encapsulating many of the ideas presented here in the *Journal of the American Psychoanalytic Association*
(Appelbaum 1966). Judging by how rarely it was cited in the
literature, the number of invitations to speak about it, and informal
observations of colleagues, it was pretty much overlooked. But one
shouldn't complain. Aristotle (McKeon 1941) had these ideas
originally, and he also had to propagate them against resistances. He
wrote, "For it is not enough to know *what* we ought to say; we
must also say it *as* we ought . . ." Persuasion is best achieved, he
said, when the persuader radiates goodness (which we can translate
as the evocativeness of "bedside manner," charisma, inspiration).
"It is, essentially, a matter of the right management of the voice
to express the various emotions . . . there are three things—
volume of sound, modulation of pitch, and rhythm—that a speaker
bears in mind . . . who usually wins prizes." And yet Aristotle

also writes, "delivery is—very properly—not regarded as an el-
evated subject of inquiry . . . we must pay attention to the
subject of delivery, unworthy though it is, because we cannot do
without it." So Aristotle, even as he was transmitting his insights,
partially shares our ambivalence about evocativeness.

To think of evocativeness in dynamic terms is for many people
somewhat more palatable than thinking of it in constitutional
terms. Dynamics, too, are deterministic, but they extend hope, the
same hope that informs and energizes the arduous self-discovery of
psychotherapy and the battle against the predetermined and constantly repeated. The analogy with art holds in this respect as well.
It is possible through analysis and other means of education to learn
to be more evocative. But before one can learn how evocative a
person can ultimately become, the task has to be approached
courageously and taken seriously enough for sustained, disciplined
thought and experiments in training.

4

Footlights and Footnotes:
Art and Psychotherapy

I t is important that the analogy I am making between art and psychotherapy not create misunderstandings about my funda-mental definition of evocativeness, especially as my remarks often refer to literary and dramatic rhetoric, so different from the more usual scientific presentation. I am *not* invoking the image of a therapist who plays to the second balcony—routinely cranking out or struggling to find utterances worthy of quotation, pursuing great moments, speaking "dramatic" language whenever possible. *Nor* am I defining the therapist as one who manipulates—in the common and heavily freighted sense of the word—the patient into a particular form of behavior or pattern of thought. The evocative therapist does not use the artful playing of roles merely for the purpose of providing the patient with a fresh chance at an old scenario, though such a corrective emotional experience is often useful. Far more subtly, the very concept of playing roles, in psychotherapy as in theater, must be understood as a process by which the evocative actor/therapist, rather than assuming or manufacturing them, discovers in himself the roles that will open the way toward the most healing insights.

Far from defining the evocative therapist as one who must consistently reach dramatic or literary heights, I define the evocative psychotherapist as one who has at his command a flexible range of responses and interventions. Evocativeness can come in all forms, from deafening silence to deafening speeches, from murmurs to marvels, from singing inspiration to demonstrations of self-control. Patients force individuality on any therapist who might otherwise adopt a one-size-fits-all approach; the roles the therapist chooses are determined by what patients bring and need. The most effective and useful way of behaving with any patient is determined by the total diagnosis of the situation—by the patient's momentary psychosexual mode, the state of the transference, the degree of resistance, the patient's particular kind of receptiveness or lack of it. Based on such a diagnosis, the evocative therapist adopts a stance whose qualities are most likely to be evocative to that particular patient at that particular time.

That I have weighted my discussion of the use of evocativeness on the side of injecting color in order to help bring the unaware usefully into awareness reflects the empirical fact that most patients usually require those steps. Patients tend as a group to overuse intellectualization and isolation of affect, and so require counteremphases by means of expressive-evocative interventions. Yet at times the most evocative intervention is the most subtle. Leston Havens (1987) supplies an example of one such instance, in which he was working with a patient who feared the challenge of uncovering the interpersonal aspects of psychotherapy.

> One day she seemed especially still and distant. I mused aloud, "What *is* one supposed to do?" To my surprise, she crisply replied, "Right!" and after a long pause, "I don't know what to do. I *never* know what to do." I had put myself in the midst of her uncertainty, verbalized it for her, and shared her desperation by my tone. At the

same time, there was no implication that she should know or decide, as many ways of calling attention to her indecision might have suggested.

Encouraged by the patient's response, Havens continued musing on what he took to be her thoughts, each time drawing her a bit more out of her shell and toward him. In so doing he was, of course, using a technique frequently used with children, who are notoriously difficult to engage in an inward-turning stance. By converting the ordinarily more active therapist into a passive one, the therapist was neutralizing some of the patient's fears. One can speculate that the patient was encouraged by the therapist's novel and continued attempts to draw her out, his patience and loyalty in doing so, his willingness to be reassuringly passive, his recognition of this need (and implied other needs), and the implicit reassurance that he, despite her devices, could understand her. He could, after all, seem to read her mind, just as she used to both fear and wish her parents could. There would be plenty of time to analyze that idealization if necessary. For the present, and in response to her immediate and paralyzing fear, how nice to have an omniscient therapist.

This understated approach can be used evocatively with a very different kind of patient as well. A person on the borderline of neurosis and psychosis, with too many ideas and feelings careening around in the mind, suffers from too much feeling, from being too aware. Evocativeness in the form of bringing more ideas and feelings into awareness would only add to the patient's sense of disorientation. Evocativeness in the form of a calming, clarifying, down-to-earth stance based in reality would be safer and more effective. The therapist would, still *by way of evocation*, erect barriers against more new ideas and feelings, and detoxify and better organize those already there. In such situations, one wants to evoke calmness, and a sense of control—the feeling of an ally who is willing and able to lend his own ego functions. Without necessarily saying it in so many words, the therapist would create a sense of "this too shall pass"—and that, however incomprehensible it may be at the moment, there is order to be found in the chaos.

This ability of the therapist to change his method to suit the specific needs of the patient, which means that the therapist is able to change his self-presentation, may create in the minds of some a semantic misunderstanding involving the term "manipulation." Evocativeness, as I define it, has nothing in common with manipulation, when that word is used to imply insincerity or some form of play-acting assumed in order to dehumanize or control others, as when one employs emotional distance masquerading as closeness. Let us examine this concern.

Manipulation, as I have mentioned, commonly refers to situations where the manipulator pursues his own ends and ignores the needs of the one manipulated. That could, of course, happen in psychotherapy, as it could in any endeavor, but it need not. To the extent that evocativeness could be seen as a kind of manipulation, manipulation should be understood in its original and pragmatic sense, as the use of the hand: one has a task, one possesses tools or methods, and one uses the best tools or methods available to get the task done. In this sense, all human interactions include manipulations. Different people want different things for themselves and others, and they set about exploring and discovering various methods for achieving these ends. As I use the word, manipulation is simply the opposite of being helpless.

Another misunderstanding that could arise from my definition of evocativeness is the confusion of role-playing as I define it with the technique of role-playing recommended by Alexander and French (1946). In this technique, as they conceived of it, the therapist artfully plays roles—consciously and designedly behaving like people significant in the patient's life—except that at key moments the therapist responds differently from the way those people of the past did. This provides the patient with what they called a "corrective emotional experience." The patient can now see his expectations as subject to change and so, therefore, his responses can change as well. In this scheme, instead of summoning (evoking) what is organically already in place (though perhaps hidden from the patient's view), the therapist places an artificial element there, one to which the patient reacts as one would expect. Such a therapist could be seen as having evoked the patient's reaction, but in my view the word properly used to cover such artificially contrived situations would not be "evocative" but "provocative." Evocativeness widens the range of participation. Provocativeness draws a circumscribed ring around the therapist's action and the patient's reaction. It narrows as it intensifies. Despite its apparent success in arranging changed behavior, provocativeness keeps the patient's deepest patterns of thought and feeling in place. Successful evocativeness brings to light endless possibilities by way of understanding—understanding of both the words and the music.

I define role-playing, as it relates to evocativeness, not as the process of taking on a role wholly separate from the self, but as consciously making use of a repertoire of selves or self-presentations that can be adopted and modified as circumstances require. In this sense, the analogy between acting and therapy is particularly useful. Both evocative actors and evocative therapists acknowledge a spectrum of genuine selves, ranging from habitual tendencies and self-presentations (what we call personality) to self-presentations markedly different from that habitual personality. The point is that the spectrum exists, and that the actor or therapist uses it self-consciously in pursuit of greater and more subtle evocativeness. What is often misunderstood, both in acting and in therapeutic circles, is the difference between acting and being. In the case of the actor, according to Stanislavski, the Russian actor and director, and Sanford Meisner (1994), among others, true evocativeness (great acting) has nothing to do with taking on the personality of another person. Rather, evocative acting means, in Meisner's words, "living truthfully under imaginary circumstances." Actors discover the role within themselves, rather than stepping outside of themselves into the role. The artful devices an actor may employ are tinsel and window dressing if the actor himself is not, in himself, deeply immersed in the role. An apt analogy from another art form is Picasso's instruction that one should eat the apple before painting it.

In the case of therapy, we can think of evocativeness in similar terms. The evocative therapist does not assume roles outside of his (wide) range of genuine selves, but rather he discovers, expands, and makes use of that range. Holding transference constant, there would be significant agreement as to what kind of *person* the therapist was—gruff, charismatic, kindly, courtly. From time to time, as circumstances require it, the therapist might exaggerate or downplay what he knows to be his usual tendencies and presentations. He might also think through his repertoire of selves to find and adopt a self-presentation quite different from "himself." In doing so, he is not being manipulative or insincere any more than the actor is. The therapist learns through diagnosis (observation and empathy cogwheeling with theory) the role that the patient is playing, with its correlated anticipations and purposes, and he adopts the attuned complementary role. The therapist does this convincingly by way of finding that role within himself—one not hoked up out of imaginative whole cloth, but one that is an expression of a part of the authentic self, as a selection from his repertoire. By way of flexibility and self-awareness, presumably greatly aided by his own self-exploratory experience, the therapist can "be" anybody. For such a therapist, "nothing human is alien."

This ability to adopt appropriate selves does not, however, require that the therapist has to have had experiences identical to those of the patient. Rather, the therapist has to have available to him an understanding of the universal qualities of the human condition. In her book on acting, Uta Hagen (1973) defines "substitution" as empathy and understanding that is based on *similarities* rather than a *duplication* of experience. An actor can play the role of Hitler by drawing upon the actor's usually latent megalomania and sadism without his having literally designed plans for world conquest and systematic murder. So, too, a therapist can empathize with states that he has not experienced. Instead, he discovers the latent qualities in himself that would help him respond with the most helpful and effective self-presentation. Just as imagination can substitute for reality, sometimes substitution can even improve upon reality for acting purposes—and for therapeutic purposes as well. For example, an actor who was in fact raped may find it difficult to play the part of a rape victim; she may be reluctant to enter imaginatively into an experience so suffused with the pain of actuality. The rape victim might be better played by an actor who can *imagine* what it would be like to be raped in the manner the playwright has written about it. Similarly, a therapist who has no personal correlative for a patient's experience might find that he can listen and respond fully, imaginatively, and evocatively using the technique of imaginative substitution. Ambrose Bierce, who fought in the Civil War, wrote less convincingly about war than did Stephen Crane, who did not fight.

When drawing upon all the selves, or roles, that therapists have available to them, are therapists "inhuman" or "inauthentic"? No, they are more human and authentic than at those times when they deny, avoid, intellectualize, and isolate out of existence their latent roles and selves. What is inhuman is the false, therapeutically irrelevant warded-off aspect of self. The self, drawn by way of evocativeness into awareness and experience, energizing the nerve endings attached to life at its most vital, is more human than most of us usually are. As the actor Stephen Fry (1997) put it with regard to his role as Oscar Wilde in the film *Wilde*: "I couldn't possibly be Wilde, but . . . I certainly feel that playing him has somehow allowed me to be more myself."

Occasionally when I present this material to colleagues one or more of them raise the question of where *accuracy* of intervention ends and the *power of evocativeness* begins. It is a good question. In the limiting case the evocative therapist can be seen merely as a purveyor who uses the artifices of the actor to persuade, with the content being treated as of little inherent value. Such a situation resembles the similarly overdrawn assertion that narrative truth rather then veridical truth is solely important. A lot of philosophizing goes into that debate. It often spills over into epistemological discussions fueled by antiauthoritarian passions, with the authority of arbiters of truth and reality summarily rejected as somehow unfair. Be that as it may, there is no getting away from the fact that people have had certain experiences in reality (never mind for the moment who is to say what reality is) and they do carry around and are influenced by fantasies about those real events. As Eissler (1967) says of *Hamlet*'s ability to move us, it is due to the play's grounding in fact, the fact of the Oedipus conflict: "No beauty of language . . . alone could achieve the effect the tragedy has had throughout many generations." It follows that the more contact with the facts and their associated feelings that the therapist can make, the more evocatively powerful and long-lasting his interventions will be.

In short, the best situation is that of a therapist who is not only skilled in learning the facts of the patient's life (the diagnostic understanding gained by way of empathy and verbal presentations amalgamated with theory), but who can also communicate that understanding evocatively. Other possibilities include those of unskilled diagnosticians who are nonetheless personally evocative, and skilled diagnosticians who are personally unevocative, with the worst situation being that of a poor diagnostician who is also unevocative. Actors need to know their lines as well as how to deliver them.

Finally, evocation can be used or misused by bad actors, in both senses of the word. These include such types as televangelists, for example, who, as events have shown, are usually in it for the money and who use their evocative skill cynically for crass manipulation of others. They also include naive and ignorant practitioners who use their evocative and often largely suggestive skills to "recover" apparent memories, heedless of their truth or falsity.

5

The Evocateur

After having discussed evocativeness in conceptual terms, I turn now to the "evocateur," the person of the therapist. On the face of it, speaking of the therapist's personality seems the obvious thing to do. Evocativeness is a personality characteristic, so naturally the person him- or herself should be an object of study. Yet a curious silence has surrounded the question of the therapist's personality. Freud (1933) made few references to the person of the analyst. He did say, however, that "Among the factors that influence the prospects of analytic treatment . . . must be reckoned . . . the individuality of the analyst."

Greenson (1972) writes that the "personality of the psychoanalyst does play a role in every psychoanalytic treatment. It is significant that this fact is well known but rarely openly discussed in the psychoanalytic literature." As Ernst Ticho (1972) writes, "The influence of the personality of the psychoanalyst on the patient's treatment is well known but rarely discussed. Follow-up studies and psychotherapy research studies say little about personality factors of the analyst." Ticho surely had in mind the Psychotherapy Research Project of the Menninger Foundation, of which he and I were members. This large, lengthy, and expensive project, which spawned many articles and books, nonetheless had relatively little to say about the overall personality of the therapist as it influenced psychotherapy. As Ticho suggests, that is another example of what seems a peculiar tendency to dismiss such a manifestly important issue. Glover's famous questionnaires, in 1928 and again in 1955, offer further evidence of this tendency. In his 1955 report, for example, he wrote that "more than half of the replies agreed that the person of the analyst plays a considerable part . . . a more important part than is always realized." Ticho, writing in 1972, believed that questionnaire answers in the 1970s would be the same. More recent professional literature continues to ignore, for the most part, the role and importance of the therapist's personality. As late as 1991, Beaudry wrote that "Normally one does not think of the character of the analyst as a component of analytic technique."

To a large extent, Ticho and Glover were observing and operating out of what is now called a one-person psychology, a model that encourages therapist behavior that can be described as having an opaque quality. Putting it in caricatured (and in my view, limited) terms, in this model the analyst merely administers a pure technique, secure in his positivistic and authoritarian philosophy. Thus, he functions in the same way with all patients. His idiosyncratic personality matters little, if at all, so there is no need to attend much to it.

The process known as two-person psychology holds a contrasting view of the therapist; in this model, he constructs more than administers, and is subject to influence and distortions of subjectivity, just as the patient is. It follows from this view that the analyst should be studied—and/or study himself—as much as the patient. The pervasiveness of this postmodernist two-person position would lead one to expect that evocativeness would finally get its due; the contemporary question of how a new emphasis on the therapist's personality might change the field is pregnant with possibilities.

Such an emphasis may still be on the way, but for now it seems to me that evocativeness continues to be markedly overlooked. The question of why this is true clamors for dynamic explanations that are more subtle than those in the dispute between one-person and two-person modes of therapy. This brings us back to the idea, some aspects of which are noted in Chapter 3, that we naturally shy away from the discovery of fundamentally distressing emotions and/or limitations. Here, Ticho (1972) usefully delineates the difference between conflict-driven behavior and that arising from character traits or personality. He says, in effect, that it is one thing to recognize conflict of a limited sort in a circumscribed sector of the personality. It is quite another to train a searching light on the whole personality, the self. That is to risk shame and humiliation, as well as the possibility of exposing one's self to the implied challenge of having to do the work of developing or enhancing one's skills.

In the interests of countering such reluctance, I here suggest some (chiefly intrapsychic) characteristics that encourage or discourage evocativeness. We begin with a detailed look at the *process* of evocativeness. And once again we turn to art for insights.

Freud (1908), Kris (1952), Beres (1957), Schafer (1983), and others have used the concept of "regression in the service of the ego" as a model for artistic creativity, and this concept is useful for understanding evocativeness as well. The phrase "regression in the service of the ego" rolls so trippingly off the tongue, making modest entry when it has every right to be announced with trumpets. It says much of what needs to be said about the psychological aspects of creativity. It gives the lie to Freud's pessimistic fear that his work failed to contribute much to the knowledge of art. It conveys cogently what in fact does take place in much creativity.

Daydreams, night dreams, humor, sexual orgasm, and Saturday night revelries are quotidian examples of our capacity to regress and progress. We are but a touch of energy away from slipping back toward the mental life of the child and flipping forward to that of the adult.

As the phrase implies, the process of regressing in the service of the ego is composed of two parts, one passive and one active. In the passive phase the artist or therapist allows or develops a passive, receptive, regressive movement toward the wellspring of the primary process. When one is "there," one is open to novel ways of thinking and feeling. One listens, allows, accepts. To an artist or therapist in this state, yes, indeed, "nothing human is alien." One takes advantage of the passive phase to empathize with the patient in order to learn, know, and sense what needs to be evoked. In this empathic act, one insinuates one's self into the psychosexual level of the patient at that moment, and follows the corresponding trails or markers of the ideas and feelings that are most operative then. That sense-knowledge informs the decision as to what to do and how to do it. This diagnostic process is a crucial first step toward evocativeness.

The active phase of regression in the service of the ego requires that something be produced from the information passively received. The evocative therapist at this point eschews passivity, strikes while the therapeutic iron is hot, does not dither. In the active phase, the evocative therapist draws upon the gathered information, amalgamates it with theoretical underpinnings, and puts ingenuity into high gear. The active phase draws upon the ego's capacities for shaping into aesthetic and communicative forms what emerges from regression. It draws upon memory, anticipation, and judgment for help with the decisions—what to say, when to say it, what tone of voice, with what emphasis, and much more. The regression is now put in the service of the ego.

It matters little whether the creative act is writing poetry, playing a jazz improvisation, or making an evocative psychoanalytic interpretation. The principle is the same. The evocative therapist, like the other creators, is required to be flexible enough to take the regressive-progressive path. That is one way of saying that the evocative therapist possesses sufficient tolerance of affect and anxiety and is sufficiently unafraid of regression to risk immersion in states of mind and feeling that have been on the whole conquered in the course of maturation and development. And out of this regressive experience the therapist must be skillful enough to make something therapeutically and evocatively useful.

So the evocative therapist must be able to negotiate the demands of the active and passive phases of the regression–progression pattern. What intrapsychic qualities are required for such a task? David Rapaport (1950) needed to learn microscopically about intrapsychic abilities in his quest to establish a psychoanalytic theory of thinking and action. He found his microscope in psychological tests. Tests offered a standardized situation, the opportunity to learn from responses to ambiguous stimuli and from performance on tasks with varying degrees of structure. With the tests he was able to get under the skin of personality, to link surface behaviors with drives, and, filtered through his own ego functions, to predict and change behavior in ways derived from this meticulous understanding. Thus was born the Rapaport-Schafer diagnostic testing tradition. In tracking down the intrapsychic elements contributing to evocativeness, we can make use of Rapaport's elegant and systematic method by examining the categories of mind delineated by the tests, categories that constitute a systematic appraisal of personality, and that can usefully be applied to the personality of both patient and therapist.

Chief among these categories is affect. Affect is the technical term, commonly translated as feelings, that refers to the basic, overall autonomic discharge facility that is part of the human equipment. The new parents' worried question, "Does the newborn have ten fingers and ten toes?" could just as easily be expressed as, "Is the newborn affectively responsive?" If that responsiveness could be called feeling at all, it would be a poorly differentiated feeling indeed. Only with maturation in a favorable environment does the raw substrate of affect become refined into feelings. The speed, quality, and extent of such refinement varies widely even as its beginnings do at birth (any neonatal observer will attest that infants differ at birth in their "emotional" responsiveness). But the vicissitudes of life and environment steadily separate people into groups having greater or lesser capacities. Some people go through life with feelings that do not develop far beyond the mass affect discharge of infancy, while others achieve an exquisite sensitivity to and expressiveness of feeling, along with the ability to control and direct their feelings.

The differences are largely caused by the family's attitudes toward having and expressing feelings. At the simplest level, a child brought up in an atmosphere of free expression of feeling learns that such expressiveness is a way of life. The general ambiance of the family is made concrete and persuasive by key individuals. For example, a mother who freely and warmly expresses feelings teaches the child to be unafraid of those sudden, imminently disorganizing, inexplicable surges of the machinery of passion. She teaches the subtleties of feelings and the opportunities that provide for pleasure. All this is a way of saying that as the vagaries of the environment interact with the primitive substrate of affect, the results are greater or lesser capacities for emotional experience and the evocative use of it.

The Rorschach test can be a useful measure of the differences in people's development and expression of feelings. Let us assume the colored areas of the inkblots represent affects. People vary greatly as to what they see in the Rorschach cards that have color in them—some people will see pleasant, muted tints ("a tawny leaf"), while others will see images of fiery intensity ("red bubbling lava"). These variations are mirrored in the real life of the personality. Thus, people who fail to notice the color can be expected to be living "colorless" lives—detached and emotionally neutral, if not outright cold. They would do well in professions that require objective decision-making or understanding, where feelings do not interfere and are not relied upon for their practice. For such people to attempt to be psychoanalysts would be a poor choice, for that profession requires feelings as its stock in trade.

Other people not only report seeing color in the Rorschach inkblots, but are floored by the experience. They may heatedly object to the color, report dizziness, turn away from the task, or show impaired judgment and diminished reality testing. A psychotherapist with such intolerance of feelings would be constantly subject to the challenge of acting impulsively when stimulated by emotion, or be striving unsuccessfully to isolate meaning from feeling.

The evocative therapist will have at his disposal a wide range of affects so that he can resonate with any in the patient's repertoire. He will be capable of shifting as the patient shifts. If he is not, the patient's emotional development will be distorted or hampered, and the two will be out of attunement. For example, should the therapist be white-hot with the experience of the moment, his evocative efforts could be rendered not only useless but ludicrous with a patient who is incapable at the time of experiencing and understanding white-hot emotions with the help of even the most evocative therapist. If, on the other hand, the therapist is emotionally isolated, the patient will learn to keep a rein on his feelings, lest *he* seem ludicrous. Matching the quantity, range, and intensity of feelings, as well as the presence of control over them provides the groundwork for evocativeness. Mismatches in any of these areas limit evocativeness.

The color-shading response is the name given in the Rorschach test to the patient's ability to combine the more simple perception of color with a perception of texture and subtle shades in that color. For instance, what one subject might call "blood" in the ordinary color response, another subject might call, in the color-shading elaboration, "dried blood" because of the ridges that this subject perceives in the shadings. Where one subject might simply see a colored textile, another subject might see a bouclé because of the nubby texture. This difference illustrates starkly the different ways in which people experience these feelings, and the extent to which people either discharge those feelings, at one end of the spectrum, or, at the other, are engulfed by them. For example, my colleagues and I (Appelbaum and Colson 1968, Appelbaum and Holzman 1962) have systematically demonstrated that, in hospitalized patients at least, there was an association between the giving of the color-shading response and suicidal behavior. Our rationale was that those who gave that response stayed with the affect experience, investigated it, and immersed themselves in the details of it, rather than simply having the emotional experience and discharging it. If that deep and detailed experience was one of misery, then that misery was maintained, and even exaggerated, without recourse to the release provided by more immediate discharge.

By contrast, some lucky people will fully register the feelings stirred by the color, allow it expression in images that resonate with passion, and then subject the perception and experience to organization, control, and modulation. These people enjoy their feelings, cogwheel them with reality, and may put them to good use. They have, one might say, a *tolerance for affects*, a key ingredient in evocativeness. One of our control groups in the 1962 study was composed of psychiatric residents, and the incidence of the color-shading response was higher in that group than in the other control groups. We speculated that the color-shading response in higher functioning "normals" represented a capacity to stay with and fully experience the emotion stirred by the color, and to put that experience to use. One constructive use for sustained emotion, especially for therapists, could be to relate ourselves to the subtle and detailed emotions of the psychotherapeutic encounter. Another use would be to guide therapist understanding by way of emotion's path, inviting greater insight. So aspects of the color-shading response seem to signal the ability to respond to and evoke what otherwise might be missed through the process of quick discharge.

The Rorschach test also can be used to measure a subject's tolerance for anxiety, and understanding this tolerance level is central to understanding the issues of evocativeness and therapeutic success. First, it is important to note the differences between anxiety and affect. To begin with, there is no correlation, as measured by the Rorschach, between the amount of a subject's affect and the amount of his or her anxiety. In our 1962 research, for example, the test results did not link anxiety and suicide as they linked color perception and suicide. The theoretical scaffolding is different as well. Anxiety seems to have its inception in the primitive need to be warned of danger: we need warning so that we can take the requisite protective steps. According to Freud, much of life is determined by the organism's need to keep anxiety at a tolerable level: a level high enough to motivate and low enough so as not to be overwhelming and excessively painful.

While the experiences of anxiety and affect are different, anxiety, like affect, does powerfully influence evocativeness and therapeutic success. Just as a subject's perception of color indicates and measures affect, the perception of achromatic shading in the inkblots indicates anxiety. Let us assume that the rather forbiddingly smeared black ink of the Rorschach blots is equivalent to a dark and forbidding forest that stands between the self and what the self wants to accomplish on the other side of the forest. If the forest is too frightening, the individual can refuse to enter it by taking the long way around or giving up on the goal. Or one can suck in one's breath and plunge ahead despite one's fears. We say that the latter approach demonstrates a *tolerance for anxiety*. The former could be said to show a low tolerance for anxiety. Psychotherapy, with its ambiguity and avowed goal of knowing what has been relegated to the unknown, is a situation of anxiety par excellence. Patients with a low tolerance for anxiety, prototypically one or another variety of addict or those who tend toward impulsive action, frequently avoid the psychotherapeutic situation through lateness and absence, ultimately to drop out. They simply cannot tolerate the anxiety. Others, who have difficulty tolerating anxiety to a lesser degree, are much more subtle in their resistance: they use avoidance mechanisms that are not so dramatic and obvious but that nonetheless can be deadly to psychotherapy and life. These patients tend to over-exercise defenses and to overcontrol anxiety. They may do that by talking only of superficial matters or, crucially and insidiously, they may appear to be doing the right things—reporting, introspecting, thinking psychologically—but underneath they are refusing to enter the forbidding forest. They withhold their emotional and intellectual participation. What should be evocative is flat. Unfortunately, there are many instances when therapists, too, do not tolerate anxiety well enough to be maximally helpful to their patients. They may join the patient in a collusion so that both of them stay out of the dark, anxious forest, on the other side of which is the necessary depth of understanding, information, and means of change that can only be gotten to by mastering anxiety.

In addition to developing appropriately empathic affective responses and a high tolerance for anxiety—both of which lay the groundwork for evocativeness—a therapist can engage a whole range of cognitive operations that can increase evocativeness in moment-by-moment interactions with patients.

In recent years the cognitive aspect of psychotherapy, by which is meant the rational pursuit of insight, has been equated with emotional coldness and a rigid adherence to theory more than to patient experience. The recent assertion that a two-person inter-active relationship is superior to a one-person intrapsychic focus also reflects that trend. Whatever the merits of the dispute, one consequence is to downplay the whole range of cognitive operations that aid or inhibit evocativeness.

One such cognitive intervention is to recognize with the patient how seemingly dissimilar thoughts or behaviors stem from the same fantasy or experience or feeling. Such a recognition requires a capacity for abstract thinking. One way to measure abstract thinking is with psychological test questions that ask how two things are alike (the "Similarities" subtest of some intelligence scales). The capacity for abstraction makes possible analogy, humor, and metaphor—all of which are evocative devices.

Another powerful intervention is the therapist's choice of words. Precise, colorful, interesting, memorable words strongly contribute to evocativeness. Facility with words depends not only upon some raw number of words available to the therapist, but also on a sensitive ear that hears them just ahead of their selection. This capacity to hear thoughts "ahead of time" enables the evocative therapist to select the words most likely to achieve the most desirable effect. All this is vocabulary in the richest sense of the word. Productivity and facility with words is the single best measure of verbal intelligence, and verbal intelligence powerfully influences the ability to do psychotherapy in general and to be evocative in particular.

To be evocative one has to construct in one's mind the scene, sound, and experience that one reverberates to, and to do so clearly enough to convey it. That requires the capacity for fantasy. Fantasy is not just the production of hypothetical ideas, though that is part of it. Fantasy is the ability to develop plots; to embellish; to imagine implications; to answer the question, "What is going on?" in all its shadings and nuances, twists and turns; to think about what it is, was, and might be. That capacity can be seen in the way people do or don't project liveliness onto the Rorschach images, embed the images in at least fragments of stories, and see the inkblots as being dynamic rather than static. Rapaport and his colleagues called this phenomenon "fabulation." Along with such related abilities as abstract thinking, fabulation contributes to psychological-mindedness, the sine qua non for successful insight-oriented psychotherapy.

Another key personality dimension involves the degree to which the therapist's ideation can be used to control behavior and so facilitate more balanced and effective cognitive interventions. The inkblots provide a measure of this in the so-called Experience Balance, a measure of the relationship between ideational capacities and affect. If a subject's responses are markedly weighted on the ideational side, the person is likely limited in the ability to infuse experience with feeling. If responses are too weighted on the color side, the person is likely subject to labile, tempestuous feeling, to thoughtless large-muscle action, or to somatization. Such action-oriented therapists might very well eschew the sometimes time-consuming organic development of evocativeness in favor of prescribing a pill—figuratively and sometimes literally. In these regards, it can only be helpful to know one's tendencies and one's constant errors, the better either to adjust them or use them.

As we can see by investigating evocativeness in terms of both inborn traits and cognitive techniques, the ability to be evocative depends upon the melding of both intrapsychic machinery and self-and-other experience. In this light, the recent opposition between such relational approaches as object-relations and self psychology and that of ego psychology can best be used as a welcome corrective to excesses in both modes. For example, rationality, insight, and cognition can correct for relational dangers of uncritical immersion in feelings, undue emphasis on "togetherness," and thoughtlessness masquerading as creative spontaneity.

With respect to ego psychology, as I have noted throughout, there is a constant danger that the application of many relatively complex psychoanalytic theories can influence the unwary toward unevocativeness, toward forgetting that the intrapsychic machinery is energized by passion. (After all, structures only come into being and continue in order to satisfy and regulate first-order, experience-near behavior.) Stimulated by competing, explicitly humanistic points of view, the evocative ego psychologist can, as the situation requires, shift the level of discourse and thinking away from abstraction and adjust his behavior to most fully encompass the subject closest at hand—the drama of the patient's life. Moreover, the therapist who has thought through the implications of ego functioning is likely to be more human than otherwise.

Ultimately, the most evocative therapist would be one likely to think less about defining and rigidly holding to a specific method, and more about working with and modifying, as needed, a method that best suits his and his patients' temperaments and capacities for understanding, giving and receiving effective interventions. To care enough to engage one's feelings with those of another, to enter another's experiential world, to face the frightening, warded-off realms of emotion with determination and skill—all these are acts of love, and are experienced as such by the patient. The evocative person is in intimate connection with love—a continuation of loving past experiences, or a powerful longing for them.

Love, however, is a suspect experience. It is soft rather than hard, artistic rather than scientific, feminine in what has been primarily a masculine world. That is one reason why love is underestimated in all healing. Working silently, it is mostly smuggled in as an aspect of suggestion and placebo. Yet the nature of healing requires the presence of love. Since love so potently energizes or discourages healing, some people get better when by all odds they should not, and others succumb when they should survive. That is, some people "understand" love and healing, while others do not. And the tradition is carried on from those who are healed to those who might become healers. Those who have been brought up with caring love have it to draw upon when they wish to heal others. Evocativeness requires at least moments of symbiosis, as when it employs empathy and attunement, both of which are modeled on the permeable boundaries between mother and child. Evocativeness demands the temporary sacrifice of self in favor of another's experience and needs. And the formulation of the nourishing psychological intervention requires that one work for the sake of another. Without the capacity for healing love, attempts at evocativeness degenerate into mere play-acting and insincerity. With the capacity for healing and love, evocativeness bridges two souls and unites them in common purpose.

6

Learning Evocativeness

Now that I have delineated the concept of evocativeness the question presents itself: What to do about it in clinical practice? Freud's complementary series provides a key starting point: the final common path of behavior is the result of constitutional or physiological givens as these interact with learning. In other words, our ability to develop evocativeness depends both on nature and nurture, as these determine who we are and who we can become.

Happily, or less happily as the case may be, how a person is constituted sets a boundary around how evocative that person can reasonably expect to be. Some therapists—some people—are "naturals"; they can hardly be prevented from being evocative. While scarcely anyone can fail to benefit from education in evocativeness (even Marlon Brando studied at the Actor's Studio), such training for naturals is more likely to be for smoothing, expansion, refinement, and grace but need not aim for wholesale change. Those people who are naturally unevocative do require wholesale change, and even when that is attempted, one's expectations of the result should be sharply limited.

By sharply limited I do not mean hopeless. I had better not, for the good of all of us. In the foreseeable future psychotherapists are going to be selected, trained, and rewarded almost regardless of their natural ability, for many other factors determine that choice and opportunity. Education in evocativeness need not aim to bridge the difference between an average expectable therapist and an ideal one, nor should it. Rather, such training should bridge the difference between the level of evocativeness a therapist begins with, and the highest level that therapist can be helped to achieve.

Not surprisingly, the key step in that direction is awareness. While formally and informally presenting this material I have been struck in particular by three things: the seeming familiarity of the concept, the quick comprehension the central idea of evocativeness receives (give or take the usual complement of resistances) and, paradoxically, a sense of its novelty and discovery. It is as if everyone has always known about evocativeness but didn't know that they knew. The extent of that not-knowing can be seen in the paucity of literature on the subject, the silence on that score in clinical discussions of patients, the ignoring of it in the selection of patients and therapists, and—it follows—the disregard of systematic training in it. Thus, we have little evidence or experience by which to measure the possibilities of education in evocativeness. And we have even less self-conscious experimentation and thought on the subject. Yet this is no time to say—as an Oscar-winning Hollywood and stage director whom I once interviewed did— that "nothing can be done" to enhance evocativeness with the few resources likely to be available in psychotherapeutic education. He himself, for example, was involved, in effect, in teaching evocativeness over a three-year academic course.

What can be done remains to be seen. First, evocativeness has to become a factor we are as aware of in the selection, training, and practice of psychotherapy, as—even—interpretation. Once an idea is in awareness, there is no telling what creative devices will enter any person's mind or be generated by the culture now newly thinking along these lines.

Freud, too, dealt with the challenges of training people to be evocative when he was formulating the requirements to become an analyst. Recognizing the difference between intellectual and emotional understanding, he chose the device of a required training analysis. In the didactic aspect of the training analysis, the psychoanalytic candidate would learn experientially what it was like to be analyzed, a substantial advantage in conducting analysis himself. In its therapeutic aspect the training analysis would "educate" the candidate in the workings of his personality, and thus provide him with opportunities to exercise freer and better choices, whether these were to select an occupation or a spouse or to make decisions that would encourage a helpful analytic process. The training analysis would overcome blind spots, would equip the patient– therapist with the courage to enter areas of life that otherwise might have been problematical to discuss and experience, and overall would introduce and encourage profundity, meaningfulness, and an existential perspective. All this would happen by engaging the candidate's feelings as well as thoughts.

Freud's sagacious understanding of the crucial interaction between feeling and thought set analysis formally on the path of empathy, emotional expressiveness, and humanism. Giving evocativeness its just due would help counteract intellectualization and tendencies toward emotional isolation as well as simply increasing the gripping power of any intervention. That power should be thought about not in terms of presence or absence but in terms of degree. In theory most of us at any given moment can be more or less expressive or evocative.

One area that Freud's model of education does not address is an awareness of the body as a tool for evocativeness. If we return to the analogy between evocativeness in psychotherapy and art, particularly the theater arts, we see with special clarity the need for such awareness. Theater art depends upon participation of the whole body in an actor's attempt to portray the whole person. Thus theater artists explicitly emphasize voice and body movement as part of their training in evocativeness.

By contrast, again taking their cue from Freud, psychotherapists mostly emphasize only one body part—the brain—to the relative exclusion of all others. Theoretically, Freud asserted the importance of the body, as in his famous statement that one day all behavior would be explainable in psycho-physical terms. Practically, he determined to unravel the mysteries of the mind solely by way of the mind. He gave up hypnosis (a sort of bypass of the mind) and corporeal touching (as in putting his hand on the patient's forehead), as he had earlier given up the belief that stimulating the body with water and fresh air could cure neuroses.

Most psychotherapists assume that a sufficient quantity and depth of insight replete with emotion and developed in a unique interpersonal relationship is sufficient to bring about change in their patients. Therefore, no specific attention to the body is or should be necessary. In general terms I agree with that formulation, but with another dimension added: that of the extent to which that recipe for change is carried out in a relationship and atmosphere of evocativeness. The problem is not whether to emphasize mind versus emphasizing body, but how to implement mind in the most helpful way—by learning and practicing all the techniques of attention and training that will enhance evocativeness. As in training that is useful for the theater, such training at times may include paying attention to the patient's and one's own voice, breathing, and posture, as these can be relevant to the evocative therapeutic task of the moment.

These days of the widening scope of treatment and of artificially imposed limits on time and activities present opportunities for just such explorations in training. These explorations can usefully combine the verbal and physical, the body and mind. Such explorations can also test among other things the hoary question, Do emotions produce ideas, or do ideas produce emotion? I offered a context for such experimentation in "Challenges to Traditional Psychotherapy from the 'New Therapies'" (Appelbaum 1982).

If for no other reason than parsimony, we need to exhaust all the creative avenues we can find in exploring, exploiting, and implementing the challenge of evocativeness as it occurs naturally—in psychotherapy and in life.

In supervising psychotherapy I have increasingly taken to modeling interventions, demonstrating to supervisees how I would intervene with patients. Here, I say in effect, are the words, tone of voice, and rhythm calculated to evoke the most desirable atmosphere for the purposes of the moment. This teaching device stems from the recognition that at any given moment the therapist is faced with numerous choices, not only about what content to intervene with (the understanding of the patient) but about the best way to intervene. As a result of this device, when facing the crucial moment of intervention with the patient, the supervisee will not only know what he wants to convey but how he wants to convey it. If I have been especially successful (evocative) in offering my interventions, the most apt therapists will have incorporated both the words and the music. Modeling will then have been replaced by identification. That would be ideal. But even at the level of merely copying, the therapist will have begun to be sensitive to the concept of evocativeness and begin to strive for evocativeness in his own work and self too.

Another device one can use for teaching is to ask the supervisee to clarify what factual understanding he wishes to convey, and then encourage the supervisee to try out several ways of communicating it. This device sensitizes the supervisee to the subtle differences available. The supervisee learns also to be flexible and creative, to recognize the valence of one word as compared to another, and to select.

One can also ask the supervisee to step into the shoes of the patient (as is done by the usual way of empathy), only this time to identify with the patient in a more systematic manner. Taking the cue from Picasso's recommendation that one eat the apple before painting it, I have the supervisee imagine he is the patient. In imagination he walks, talks, thinks, feels, looks like the patient. As the "patient," the supervisee offers his views as to what he can listen to and what he can't, what he wants to hear and what he thinks he ought to want to hear, what might make a lasting difference, and how the "therapist" seems to him as a person as well as a therapist. Walking in the steps of another tends to make of "I–you" an "I–thou."

PART II

THE CLINICAL CRUCIBLE

7

The Clinician as Critic

The first section of this book has presented evocativeness in theoretical and definitional terms. In this second section, I offer transcripts of clinical sessions and analyze these transcripts in terms of the therapist's successful and less successful uses of evocative interventions.

The greatest truth, for clinicians, lies in the clinical crucible. Yet the clinical crucible, as all scientists know, provides a particular sort of evidence. Those who require of science empirical data, citations of reliability and validity, and control groups will not find them here. I am the sole observer and judge of these clinical examples, and I have an ax to grind. I fervently believe in the truth and usefulness of the concept of evocativeness and in that sense I can be its best advocate—but for the same reason I cannot be impartial or entirely objective. The validity of my inferences, and the conclusions drawn from them, are only as good as I am as a clinician. My characterization of this work as scientific rests on a liberal interpretation of science. I share this interpretation with that of Freud, when he declared the psychoanalytic situation to be his laboratory, and acted as both investigator and therapist. So the truth of my inferences and reconstructions can never be known in any absolute sense. Here, as with inferences and reconstructions in therapy, we depend for confidence on coherence rooted in theory, logic, internal consistency, the apparent consequences of interventions, and overall feel. It is just those considerations—and disciplined thought—that distinguish clinicians on the uneasy boundary between the clinic and the laboratory.

I am defining as *data* my inferences about what is likely to have occurred in the hearts and minds of practitioners and patients at a particular moment. I had access only to fragments of the therapy transcripts themselves; I know only the words that reportedly passed between the participants. As I have noted, many more factors can, do, and should influence evocativeness: tone of voice, facial expression, and other nonverbal factors such as dress and office furnishings, among other sources of the therapist's self-presentation.

It is as if we had to judge the likely impact of a play only by reading the script. As many a bruised financial investor and artistically wounded producer, director, and actor knows, it is difficult to judge the reception of a play or film just by reading the script. Indeed, scripts are designed to leave room for interpretation. Actually, the task here is even more problematical. The transcripts are incomplete; I did not get a chance to read the whole script. Wholes can influence parts; context can determine meanings. My inferences would likely be more accurate—and fewer Broadway plays would fail—if more information about the production could be made available at the beginning. But the show must go on.

One can also raise objections with respect to my seating myself as the judge. One person's smash hit is another's bust. To put it mildly, art critics often disagree. What is evocative to one person may not be for another. The doctrine of individual differences colors all, and one can only accept that as a fact of life, whether in art or in psychotherapy. And yet there are Tonys and Pulitzers and Oscars, however imperfectly providing a sense of agreement, a rank ordering of value. Not every entry or interpretation has an equal chance of winning or of being mutative. Yet the gambler would have a far better shot at finding financial backing, enjoying or learning from a Tennessee Williams play than one cranked out by Uncle Ted in his attic office. The odds of help with one's life would be much better if one selected a therapist from recommendations of others rather than by pointing one's finger at the Yellow Pages. In the midst of uniqueness and individuality there is a sort of consensus. It is that capacity for implicit consensus on which we depend in considering the examples and judgments of evocativeness presented here.

The language of the verbatim accounts is occasionally awkward, in some cases because speech is simply less polished than edited writing, and in some because English is the therapist's second language. I pretty much have let the accounts stand unedited, since I assume that dynamics and atmospheric detail may have influenced the choice of language, and I want these influences, through the unedited words, to remain part of the record.

A word of warning. In presenting this material to audiences, classes, and supervisees—indeed, when I first realized its implications myself—I came to understand how daunting the challenge to be evocative can be. All of a sudden, even skilled veteran psychotherapists were finding that understanding and careful articulation were not enough. Now each choice of word, the tone of voice, the timing, and every detail of the surroundings was an opportunity—or a potential pitfall. Suddenly, in the midst of great potential for growth, there was new potential for failure. The faint of heart shy away from that self-confrontation. And in the demanding, difficult world of psychotherapy we are all—or should be at times—faint of heart. Only with a second look, when acclimated, was I able to counter dismay with greater recognition of the opportunity evocativeness brings to us. As with character analysis of patients, one must first become aware in order to locate what is or can be made ego-dystonic, and only then set off on the path toward change.

8

Freud's Analytic Terrain

FREUD'S "PSYCHOANALYTIC" TECHNIQUE

Sigmund Freud is the first analyst whose work I have chosen to analyze from the standpoint of evocativeness. I do this not because Freud's work represents a model of evocativeness, or because it represents a model of psychoanalytic technique to the extent that we can conventionally define it. And because the work presented is for illustrative, educative, and heuristic purposes, in principle any transcript of any psychotherapy should suit the purpose. And I have my doubts about preoccupation with Freud: it can take on the quality of cultism and uncritical fealty. Such work can be read as if it were motivated by voyeurism, even a taste for gossip. Often enough it is an attempt to discredit the work by casting doubt on the worker, whether this be done by outright enemies, or by the subtle exercise of ambivalence by putative followers. Worst of all, the citation of Freud may encourage the tendency to let him be the last word, as if "Freud said it" constituted proof rather than simply an observation: an observation that, taken in context, has more or less veracity.

Yet I have in part chosen to analyze Freud's therapy out of a deep sense of history. Freud as a source commands our respectful attention. Everybody writing in the field of psychoanalysis refers to, and uses, Freud; he is a historical fact of our intellectual life, the source from which, to put it mildly, the world has learned a great deal and continues to learn—so *not* investigating his treatment in terms of evocativeness would leave a scholarly and historical gap. Also, Freud is for many people, myself included, a source of inspiration, a role model. How he worked—issues of gossip, voyeurism, and cultism aside—is a matter of interest. For some purposes other than the one at hand, it might be useful to separate the attention to Freud's work from Freud the person. But the investigation of evocativeness prohibits drawing such a hard-and-fast distinction: one is evocative through the self, not merely through one's technical maneuvers.

I have put quotation marks around "psychoanalytic" in the heading for this section to indicate the many questions we continue to have about what constitutes psychoanalytic technique, or indeed what constitutes psychoanalysis. To take the limiting case, there are those who, at least speaking loosely, might refer to the way in which Freud conducted his self-analysis as an example of psychoanalytic technique. Others fail to make a distinction between Freud's (and Breuer's) pre-psychoanalytic case reports and the later ones. Thus, for some, the shambles of the Dora case indicate and represent the characteristics and failures of psychoanalysis as properly used and later developed. Even the later and more contemporary versions of psychoanalytic technique have regularly been subject to the damning epithet, "It's not *real* psychoanalysis." As we shall see, Freud's work with patients, especially the earlier ones, was more in the service of constructing and validating theory than it was a purely therapeutic enterprise, and therefore it presents a unique picture of psychoanalytic technique.

I could justifiably also put quotation marks around "technique" where Freud is concerned. In examining Freud's practice, one confronts the awkward realization that what Freud *did* with patients was remarkably different from what he *recommended* should be done. The evidence for this tendency runs throughout his own reports, and is confirmed and extended by his patients: he consistently ignored the basic rules of psychoanalytic technique as embodied in his brilliant, prescient series of technique papers written from 1911 through 1915. I use the word "ignored" advisedly: he did not merely take a different course of action from what he recommended, but he even failed to take his own recommendations much into consideration. He offered little in the way of explanation or deliberations about what technically he was doing and why it dovetailed, or more usually failed to dovetail, with his treatment behavior. He *ignored* his prescriptions and proscriptions. Such schisms between what is taught and what is practiced are ubiquitous in psychoanalysis (as well as other disciplines). So too, are the inevitable variations introduced by individual differences in the style and personalities of analysts. So what *is* "psychoanalytic technique?"

"The answer is the disease of the question," says André Gide by way of a lecture by Wilfred Bion. There is no technique in the sense of an agreed-upon, homogenous way; there are, however, principles of technique, based in theory—things to do or not do—that are sufficiently practiced by therapists as to permit one to orient oneself to the general area of behavior labeled (largely for convenience) "psychoanalytic technique." Paradoxically, in some ways, it is a rigid technique that makes room for numerous variations.

In assessing Freud as an evocative therapist, one encounters another set of clashing contradictions. He gives evidence of being unevocatively intellectualized, impatient, contentious, and authoritarian, and yet there is evidence also of his evoking the warmest kind of respect and admiration by way of his sensibilities and manner. Before turning to the direct data of his work with patients, I will present some of Freud's patients' impressions of the person Freud appeared to be, as these impressions have a direct bearing on the question of his evocativeness.

Concerning the general atmosphere that Freud created around him, Sergius Pankejeff, the man we know as the Wolf Man (Oberholzer 1982), wrote that "he was a fascinating personality. . . . he had a magnetism . . . an aura that was very pleasant and positive. He was witty, a very intelligent man. . . ."

The Wolf Man goes on to emphasize that Freud's personal attractiveness was so powerful that

I had the impression that Freud had a special gift for finding a happy balance in everything he undertook. This characteristic expressed itself also in the appearance of his home. . . . I can remember . . . his two adjoining studies, with the door open between them and with their windows opening on a little courtyard. There was always a feeling of sacred peace and quiet here. The rooms . . . in no way reminded one of a doctor's office but rather of an archaeologist's study. Here were all kinds of statuettes and other unusual objects which even the layman recognized as archaeological finds from ancient Egypt. . . . on the walls were stone plaques representing various scenes of long-vanished epochs. A few potted plants added life to the rooms, and warm carpet and curtains gave them a homelike note. Everything here contributed to one's feeling of . . . being sheltered from one's daily cares. . . . His purely human influence on his patients . . . was bound to be profound and lasting. Even Freud's sharp way of expressing his opinion . . . afforded one great enjoyment. Freud's appearance was such as to win my confidence immediately. He was then in his middle fifties and seemed to enjoy the best of health. . . . the most impressive feature was his intelligent dark eyes, which looked at me penetratingly but without causing me the slightest feeling of discomfort. His correct, conventional way of dressing, and simple but self-assured manner, indicated his love of order and his inner serenity. Freud's whole attitude, and the way in which he listened to me, differentiated him strikingly from his famous colleagues . . . in whom I had found such a lack of deeper psychological understanding.

The Wolf Man had given up his planned journey to meet an analyst because Freud had made such a favorable impression upon him. He felt that he had finally found what he had so long been looking for.

Echoing the Wolf Man's impressions is a comment by Mark Brunswick (Ruitenbeek 1954), son of David and Ruth Brunswick. Even after detailing many of what he considered to be Freud's errors with him and with his parents, Brunswick nonetheless says, "It was when one was in Freud's presence, looking at his deeply piercing brown eyes, which were 'almost melodramatic,' that one could detect the founder of psychoanalysis."

Similarly, Freud's analysand, Hilda Doolittle (Holland 1954), reports the battles she had with Freud while at the same time giving eloquent praise for his gifts of language—gifts that she, a poet, was particularly attuned to. "The beautiful tone of his voice had a way of taking an English phrase or sentence out of its context, you might say, of the whole language" so that the word took on special overtones and a whole new life. The analysis seems to have proceeded much more by this kind of exploration of connotation and association than by ideas about symbols or theory. "He himself—at least to me personally—deplored the tendency to fix ideas too firmly, to set symbols, or to weld them inexorably" (1973). Contradicting the frequent citations of Freud being authoritarian, Doolittle (Holland 1954) writes that Freud behaved "as if my feelings, my discoveries, were on a par with his own." Doolittle goes on to comment that when Freud spoke it was

> as if he had dipped the grey web of conventionally woven thought into a vat of his own brewing—or held a strip of that thought, ripped from the monotonous faded and outworn texture of the language itself, into the bubbling cauldron of his own mind in order to draw it forth dyed blue or scarlet, a new colour to the old grey mesh, a scrap of thought, even a cast-off rag that would become hereafter a pennant, a standard, a sign again, to indicate a direction or, fluttering aloft on a pole, to lead an army.

How wonderfully evocative Freud appears to his patient observers—physically, in his surroundings, and in his choice and delivery of words. This was at least true of those patients who idealized him and were themselves capable of highly evocative functions.

It is difficult to believe that this is the same man who is characterized as having "a merciless eye" toward others as well as himself (Kanzer and Glenn 1980). As we shall see, there is little evidence of this imaginative and poetic mind—little scarlet raised from grey—in Freud's own reports of his treatment behavior. Nonetheless, it is valuable to study Freud's own accounts of his treatment behavior, often apparently so unevocative, for several reasons. I do so partly to correct the still-pervasive criticism of Freud's technique as a seamless whole rather than a technique that changed as his theory changed, and as his experience with patients and with life changed. For example, some of those who criticize his work with the Rat Man overlook the fact that the Rat Man's treatment took place in 1907, while Freud's codification of his knowledge of technique was not published until more than five years later. At the same time, at least some of Freud's emphases and aspects of his technical stance persisted even as his theory and experience changed. He never fully gave up the emphasis on the determining effect of early trauma, for example, and his work often featured an almost relentless search for such determining memories (Ellman 1991). He continued to be at least as much an investigator as a therapist.

As we turn our attention to these accounts, it would be good to remind ourselves again that what appears on the printed page can have only an imperfect resemblance to what actually took place. We know only what Freud reports directly, or what we can glean from the reporting of others. We do not know *how* things were conveyed—the central element in the idea of evocativeness. Moreover, what the therapist thinks the therapist conveys may only imperfectly correspond to what the patient receives.

Just as disagreements regularly arise at case presentations even when the attendees are colleagues of similar seniority and theoretical leanings, so there will inevitably be disagreements about the inferences that I will be drawing. To draw inferences, especially about the unconscious and its vicissitudes, is of course to skate on thin ice. But even thin ice can support appropriate weight.

The following cases are from the pre-psychoanalytic period, both chronologically and in Freud's thinking. They bear little resemblance to psychoanalysis as it is known and practiced today, or even when the twentieth century turned, and Freud brought together the early discoveries into a functional whole, as revealed in his technique papers.

The customary therapies of the time included the use of water, massage, gentle touching, electrical stimulation, and the giving of advice and encouragement, often with a moralistic tone. Freud reports using all of these but with the crucial addition of hypnosis. With hypnosis as his main investigative tool he pursued the memories that were supposedly producing his patients' symptoms. Freud says little about the relationship between therapist and patient and nothing of the niceties of evocativeness.

What is especially intriguing to a student of evocativeness, however, are those passages between himself and his patients that are seminal to the creation of the later formulations and therapeutic practice. Freud was clearly energized by his hypotheses, by their confirmation or disconfirmation, and seemingly indifferent to the patients, as if they were mere carriers of his needed information. Nevertheless at times his recognition of human interaction and of ways to use that recognition for therapeutic purposes shines through. For example, he was acutely aware of what kind of persona he was adopting for individual patients and situations. With Emmy von N he tells of his decision not to be authoritarian, as a means of encouraging her freedom of expression. He also tells us that he countered her reluctance to take his advice this way: "I *pretended* [author's italics] to give up my proposal." He was onto the use of the voice as an important factor in evocativeness: "I asked her in an apparently innocent voice. . . ." These examples suggest a flexibility, openness, and sensitivity to himself as a key therapeutic instrument. In writing of Elisabeth von R, Freud all but uses the word evocativeness in his description of how the analyst uses himself, in this instance to overcome resistances: "The interest shown in her by the physician, the understanding of her which he allows her to feel and the hopes of recovery he holds out to her—all these will decide the patient to yield up her secret" and "This process of abreaction certainly did her much good. But I was able to relieve her still more by taking a friendly interest in her present circumstances."

Following are brief notes on the pre-psychoanalytic cases, notes selected for their at least nascent applicability to present psycho-analysis and evocativeness.

FRAULEIN ANNA O

At least on the basis of what Breuer and Freud tell us of Breuer's treatment of Anna O, Breuer was not so much unevocative as he was anevocative. The model that Breuer used—hypnotizing the patient in order to help her to bring thoughts to mind that had led to her symptoms—was a quintessential one-person model: Breuer tells nothing about their relationship, or even of any verbal interventions that he made. Indeed, when Anna O told him of her sexual interest in him, he abandoned the whole project and even withheld publication of the case. We can only speculate what was transpiring emotionally between Breuer and Anna O, what thoughts each may have had, for example, upon noticing the swelling of breasts and genitals against clothing. Yet, was there not something evocative of the patient's feelings and thoughts in Breuer's obvious attention and interest, the repeated sessions he held with Anna O, the soothing voice characteristic of many hypnotic inductions? Breuer avows that he did not use suggestion. He was, of course, referring to direct suggestion, made consciously and advisedly. He overlooks the persuasive power of indirect suggestion, and what the patient made of his behavior, whether or not Freud had any inkling of it, to say nothing of consciously employing it. In sum, this situation provides an example of evocativeness in the form of suggestion, though we do not know about any specifically evocative and interpersonal interventions that the therapist made.

FRAU EMMY VON N

Maybe it was Frau Emmy von N's occasional feistiness that stimulated Freud to make somewhat more conscious use of himself with her. He notes that he told her a white lie in order to calm her (which it did). He made magical omnipotent promises to her such as promising, while she was under hypnosis, to regulate her menstrual cycle. He tells her that she ought to believe his description of the way an asylum is run rather than another's description. He interrupts her once to show her that her fears are groundless; once again, to stop what he anticipated would be a long, useless recounting, and once more when he thought she was finished talking (and she was not). Here and elsewhere he radiates authority if not authoritarianism. His creation of an image of authority reaches its apogee when, during an argument over the veracity of one of his interpretations, he gives her twenty-four hours to agree with him, or, presumably, he will be rid of her.

One wonders to what extent this image was designed for its suggestive power, or other dynamic reasons, or, as some would aver, it was merely a natural expression of his personality. Interrupting can be used evocatively to dramatize the importance of something, the message being that it is so important it can't wait, and it is more important than what the interruptee is saying. Interrupting could also be a function of narcissism, poor control over impulses, or just bad manners. With these cases I did, however, get an almost palpable sense of Freud's busy mind developing strategies, among other things trying to find evocative ways of pursuing his and the patient's ends. My image is of bits of brilliance, empathy, and wisdom, surfacing as if following some will of their own, there but as yet unintegrated. Freud wonders, finally, whether her apparent success in the treatment is due to his suggesting the symptom away, or whether her apparent cure comes from their having investigated the cause of the symptom by way of insight. Throughout the rest of his career, right up to and including "Analysis Terminable and Interminable" of 1937, he notes that insight is not identical to cure. Perhaps the understanding that eluded him here was the role played by evocativeness, which all along could have been both facilitating and inhibiting change. Its absence could be one explanation for insight not equaling cure.

MISS LUCY R

Freud gives the patient an interpretation that takes up ten lines of the text. Its main point is a description of the Oedipus complex as it applies to her. The interpretation's only claim to evocativeness is its weight—the implication that something this lengthy and complex must be important. At its end Freud does recognize, in effect, her shame at her oedipal involvement, a beginning of an evoked experience that unfortunately only comes at the end.

She reacts to the long interpretation in her "usual laconic fashion." Freud is disappointed in that he expected that this "discussion would bring about a fundamental change in her condition." After prescribing hydrotherapy, he "insisted that she try to remember under the pressure of my hand." As an apparent result this nine-week treatment ended successfully. Was this due to the hydrotherapy, the content and insight that came to awareness and was discussed during the nine weeks, or was it Freud's hand on her head, which he used to get unconscious material? Apparently outside of his awareness was that the meaning of touch to the patient, what it evoked, may have been curative itself. As with medicine, the way touch heals can be influenced by how it is given. What feelings did Freud have about what he was doing, and what feelings did the patient have in response to his doing it, and to his stopping doing it? Why did he choose this patient and this particular time? Surely other patients at other times also complained that they could not remember, but he did not use these or other measures. In this case report, Freud ignores these textures of the situation, as they were determined by the feelings and thoughts of the participants, and as he may in his best laboratory manner have done with the patient.

KATHERINE

In reporting on Katherine, Freud makes this statement: "a girl's anxiety is a consequence of the horror by which a virginal mind is overcome when it is faced for the first time with the world of sexuality." To deal with that horror and the resistance raised by it, Freud employs a direct interpretation. His interpretation uses just the right combination of humility and decisiveness; it is neither wishy-washy nor authoritarian: "If you don't know, I'll tell you how *I* think you got your attacks. At that time, two years ago, you must have seen or heard something that very much embarrassed you, and that you'd much rather not have seen."

During this time in his development of psychoanalysis, Freud was still preoccupied with the recovery of traumatic memories, and he comments, "she was not in a position to recognize construction of a sexual incident as something that she had experienced." He says that he believes hypnosis would be required to bring that full recognition about. Without denigrating the use of hypnosis, at least under certain circumstances, we can consider that greater evocativeness might have accomplished that. Through the therapist's evocative interventions she could have been led to deal not only with a "sexual incident" but with the whole panoply of feelings and fantasies stimulated by sexuality that needed to be brought to vibrant and workable awareness. That, of course, would have required a lot more time than the single hour allotted to them. As it was, Freud's evocation of an accepting, matter-of-fact, workmanlike interest accomplished a great deal. The "virginal mind" was enabled successfully to deal with what in less intuitive, less skilled hands might have confirmed her fears, might have been in fact "a horror."

FRAU ELISABETH VON R

With respect to this patient, Freud turns a therapeutic corner: he moves from depending on the recovery of memories, with their strangulated affect, to recognizing specifically the good that can come from emotional relationships formed in the present, particularly with one's therapist: "The process of abreaction certainly did her much good. But I was able to relieve her still more by taking a friendly interest in her present circumstances."

Rather apologetically Freud comments that his case reports are "short stories . . . they lack the serious stamp of science." It is well known that Freud was exceedingly concerned that his discoveries be considered scientific—an understandable position in view of his training and the culture of the time. The tension felt between scientific and literary writing, a tension more broadly contained in his personality, is openly expressed here. He slows his usually unrelenting pursuit of early memories and experiences the better to recognize and use the effect one person can have on another. It is but a short step from here toward conceptualizing or intuiting evocativeness.

A CASE OF HYSTERIA (DORA)

The turn of the century Dora case (Freud 1905) can, of course, hardly be considered an example of good psychoanalytic technique or even an example of what we now consider to be psychoanalysis: the treatment was conducted without the benefit of free association and transference. After only three months the patient left Freud precipitously and unhappily as the result of what we would now view as a series of technical errors. The troubles that Freud got into with this patient are generally considered to be the result of his not knowing at the time how to use transference, or indeed, without even knowing what it was. The Dora case deserves to be a classic because of its historical importance; it led, among other discoveries, to the discovery of transference. That is the conventional view of the case. But, according to Patrick J. Mahoney (1982), a major scholar of Freud's case summaries, Freud's lack of knowledge about transference was not the only reason for the failure of the treatment. In Mahoney's view, Freud so disliked Dora that his feelings made it impossible for him to be empathic with her, to evoke any more from her than evidence for his theories. "His attitude," says Mahoney, "resembled that of nineteenth century parents who hardly recognized the independent identities of their adolescent children. Sometimes Freud comes across less like a therapist than like an exasperated parent with a rebellious teenager . . . he badgered her."

Mahoney generally depicts Freud as attacking Dora, giving her no credit, asserting his superior knowledge, triumphing over her—all of this motivated by Freud's "loathing for the hypocritical society ladies of Vienna," apparently an extension of his alleged misogyny. Not only that, but he used "dry" technical language.

Yet there are also some significant indications in this case that Freud was beginning to recognize the power, plasticity, and importance of words, and the incipient influence that the personality of the therapist could exert. In one comment to Dora, Freud says "I would like you to pay close attention to the exact words you used.

We may have to come back to them . . . I laid stress on these words because they took me aback. They seemed to have an ambiguous ring about them." Note Freud's sensitivity and tactfulness with regard to sexual words: As he describes the interaction, "[I questioned her] very cautiously . . . [I took] great pains not to introduce her to any first facts in the area of sexual knowledge . . . I did not call a thing by its name until her allusions to it had become so unambiguous that there seemed very slight risk in translating them into direct speech." He explains this approach in scientific terms: he did not want to introduce anything from his mind, but rather to learn things from her. Once again, his exploratory impulse is of paramount importance. But it is likely that at some level he was aware that he had an evocative job to do: "The best way of speaking about such things is to be dry and direct . . . I call bodily organs and processes by their technical names." So Freud could have consciously chosen dry, direct language in order to evoke the necessary calmness and matter-of-factness that would contribute to the therapeutic process with Dora. In criticizing Freud's use of language out of hand, Mahoney, in this instance, may very well have overlooked Freud's evocative strategy.

Elsewhere in the Dora report we learn that Freud (1905) sensed something of the possibilities in using one's self evocatively: he wondered

> Might I perhaps have kept the girl under my treatment if I myself had acted a part, if I had exaggerated the importance to me of her staying on, and shown a warm personal interest in her—a course which, even after allowing for my position as her physician, would have been tantamount to providing her with a substitute for the affection she longed for.

After acknowledging that he doesn't know the answer to that question, he goes on to say, "I have always avoided acting a part, and have contented myself with practising the humbler arts of psychology." Here Freud is being a bit disingenuous. After all, he was not averse to telling a white lie and making omnipotent promises, as he did with Emmy von N and the Rat Man. As discussed here earlier, there is a fine but important line between a strategic use of the self based on an understanding of the patient, and "acting a part." Here he correctly indicts any tendency to use evocativeness for insincere play-acting. He seems at least dimly aware that if he had evocatively communicated to the patient the importance of their relationship to one another—that is, merely adopted the clinical stance and a reassuring interpersonal atmosphere—she might have forgiven him his technical lapses. What she could not forgive was his lack of consistent empathy and human self-presentation, which in principle he could have evocatively summoned for her.

THE RAT MAN

Diagnosis has never been the strong suit of psychoanalysis, and Freud certainly didn't focus on diagnosis at the time he treated the Rat Man. Yet Freud seems to have sensed enough about the sources of the Rat Man's phobias (this was before ego psychology) to understand that the Rat Man's treatment would require unconventional measures. He did a great many things in the course of this treatment that elsewhere he clearly advises should not be done according to the proper conduct of analysis. (Freud laid down his technical rules specifically for the conduct of *psychoanalysis*, and not for any other kind of therapy.)

In treating the Rat Man, Freud freely violated the rules of

abstinence, neutrality, and incognito. He fed the Rat Man, sent him a postcard, and reassured him, in so many words, that he had a good opinion of him. Freud urged him to confront his phobia, pressured him to tell his girlfriend's name and to bring Freud a picture of her, and Freud spent a good bit of their time together lecturing and educating his patient. He claimed to do his intellectual explaining not to convince the patient, but to warm the situation, get the material going, open doors, stimulate thought—as he put it "to bring the repressed complexes into consciousness, to set the conflict going in the field of conscious activity, and to facilitate the emergence of fresh material from the unconscious."

According to some critics, although Freud's literal actions were unconventional, his impulses are consonant with psychoanalytic technique. Kestenberg (1980) offers an apologia for Freud's work with the Rat Man: Freud conveyed to the patient his own sense of conviction, his own assurance, which contrasted with and neutralized the Rat Man's excessive doubting. Freud "gave free vent to his own maternalness when he fed the hungry patient or praised him . . . a kindly, permissive quasi-maternal attitude. . . ." Kestenberg claims that this "quasi-maternal attitude" has remained the basic psychoanalytic stance. In a sense she is right. There is indeed something maternal in the caretaking clinical attitude, in the acceptance and safety a patient can expect to find in that little corner of the careering world.

From the point of view of evocativeness, however, another element comes into play, and that element is sensitivity to the patient's uniquely individual needs. An evocative therapist wishes to convey, at any given moment, to any given patient, what that particular patient might need—which may or may not include maternal care. And certainly, with a properly chosen analytic patient, one would not cross the boundaries that Freud crossed with the Rat Man. Even when we take on the task of creating a maternal environment, we hope these days to achieve that "atmosphere of safety" (Schafer 1983) and "holding" (Winnicott 1958) analytically—that is, through discussion and understanding rather than such concrete and intimate actions as Freud's. If Freud had been fully aware and trained in the powers of evocativeness, he might have trusted the analytic relationship more, and his impulses to action less.

THE WOLF MAN

The Wolf Man case is the only extended case summary that Freud published after the publication of his technique papers. If Freud had conformed to his technical rules in his treatment of the Wolf Man, then the conundrum of his unconventional behavior with previous patients would be solved: before the Wolf Man, he simply hadn't learned the rules. Yet such is not the case. In his work with the Wolf Man, Freud flagrantly disregarded his own technical prescriptions and proscriptions though he knew better. He gave money regularly to his patient, apparently out of sympathy for the man's straitened circumstances. He asked for a gift upon termination. And he set a firm ending date in an attempt to force an improvement in the process. The conundrum remains.

There is, however, much in this case that suggests Freud's instinctive gift for evocativeness. At times, the instinctiveness of this gift could be dangerous. One such instance, which nonetheless turned out well, involved Freud's promise, given to assuage the Wolf Man's doubts about analysis, that his patient would recover completely from his intestinal complaint. We can surmise that Freud substituted for analysis, at that juncture, his old friend suggestion; and we can guess further that another therapist, or Freud on a different day, might well not have achieved such a salubrious result. Freud was playing a dangerous game with such omnipotent promising. If the patient had not given up his symptom, Freud could have looked foolish, and the relationship could have been undermined. As it happens, however, the Wolf Man did indeed recover, and Freud "had the satisfaction of seeing [the Wolf Man's] doubt dwindle away." In order to trade on the patient's nascent infantile belief in the omnipotence of parents, Freud drew upon his ability to evoke that boundless faith. He most likely issued his promise with infectious confidence.

An instance of Freud's intuitive evocativeness in his work with the Wolf Man involves a subtle choice of words. Freud compliments the Wolf Man on his intelligence: he called him a "thinker of the first rank." The patient says the remark "filled me with no little pride, since in my childhood I had suffered from competition with my sister, who was two and a half years older than I and far ahead of me." Was Freud's phrase a lucky guess, a consciously chosen statement, or a beautifully intuitive flash? He could have complimented the Wolf Man's intelligence in many different ways, but he chose words that raised the Wolf Man to the "first" rank, thus elevating him above his older sister. So the Wolf Man got more than just narcissistic pleasure from the compliment. He got triumph. Whether consciously intended or not, Freud's comment evoked a major dynamic within the patient's family history, one that could be experienced and worked with. Serendipitous or not, his words are a beautiful piece of evocation.

In another instance, Freud's choice of words is far more risky. In response to the Wolf Man's raising doubts about the analysis, Freud says, "Don't start that. Because the moment you try to view things critically, your treatment will get nowhere. I will help you, whether you believe in it or not." The likely consequence of Freud's remark is that this or any patient might feel that he has to be careful of what he says. The therapist has actively threatened him with the failure of the treatment if he is not careful, implying with this threat that he no longer is free to say whatever is on his mind, if he ever was, for he could lose the therapist's love. In this case, however, the Wolf Man accepts this, and stops criticizing and doubting because, he says, he is afraid of the treatment's failing, of "getting nowhere." What may have been helpfully evocative here was Freud's decisiveness. Perhaps with all or most patients, but certainly with obsessive patients such as the Wolf Man, there can be something gripping, attention-getting, and memorable in such directness and clarity. Many therapists consistently make the error of being mealy-mouthed, of losing themselves in their own obsessive-compulsive tendencies; they are unable to master the art, or grasp the artistic usefulness, of the simple declarative sentence. It could be that such strength and simplicity gave Freud's statement its evocative power.

It also could be that the power came from Freud himself, and that he could get away with the implied threat, and even turn it to good advantage, because he was Freud. We know from the Wolf Man's comments elsewhere that he was taken by Freud the person and Freud the icon. He admired Freud's personal appearance, house, and furnishings. We have seen that evocativeness in therapy, as in the theater, can be enhanced by the staging. The question for other therapists is whether the evocativeness inherent in Freud's force and directness here can compensate for the risk of frightening the patient and undermining or distorting the relationship.

In a final example, Freud's intervention is so omnipotent and ominous that it serves best as an example of evocativeness gone awry. The Wolf Man reports that after the death of his father, Freud said, "You were lucky that your father died, otherwise you would never have become well." In reporting this intervention, the Wolf Man interpolates, "You see, I just remembered that he said that." Clearly Freud's remark, remembered decades later, was memorably evocative. But what it evoked is the question. Although the formal treatment was over, and the Wolf Man had come to Freud out of temporary grief and need, one would expect that (in addition to respecting the requirements of simple humanity) Freud would formulate his interventions with good psychoanalytic understanding and technique in mind. Yet in many respects, he gave at this sensitive time an awful intervention. Freud seems to have harkened back to the theory of seduction: the actual event was the determining factor, not the meaning and fantasies attached to it. Freud seems to have held the actual death of the father to be so influential that without the event, the patient would not have become well. Once again, we have Freud asserting that such-and-such a condition must be met for the patient to maximally benefit from the treatment. The putative gain for the Wolf Man—or any patient—would have to be great indeed to be worth such a threatening and insensitive intervention.

SUMMARY

The specific cases that Freud chose to write about were not exceptional: many of his characteristics appear and reappear in reports by both his analysands and others (Roazen 1995). One example is the treatment of David Brunswick. Freud treated Brunswick from 1927 to 1930, and as late as that Freud was breaking his own rules—in this instance, he was treating members of the same family. (We know, of course, that in what was perhaps his most unconventional activity he treated his own daughter, Anna). Freud's treatment of the Brunswick family demonstrates that the inconsistencies between his theory and his practice do not, in fact, represent merely his stumbling early attempts to teach himself analytic technique. Mark Brunswick, David's son, had a seven-year analysis with Freud beginning as late as 1924, which, according to David, featured many of the same deviations from the technique Freud professed that others had noted through the years.

In *Freud as We Knew Him* (Ruitenbeek 1954), Joseph Wortis reports in some detail what it was like to be a patient of Freud's. The treatment, a brief psychotherapy, took place in 1934, when Freud was 78. According to the patient, Freud was at his pedantic, opinionated, and rule-breaking worst. He broke boundaries by taking the patient's time in order to satisfy his own curiosity about Havelock Ellis. He criticized the patient for not talking clearly and loudly enough, and did so "petulantly," without acknowledging the possibility that his own hearing difficulty might have been the cause of the problem. He admonished the patient with, "You ought to break yourself of those habits (scratching of the head and cleaning of nails). You must learn to absorb things and not argue back. And, I told you once before, it is your narcissism, your unwillingness to accept facts that are unpleasant." By now this is not an unfamiliar tone.

Norman N. Holland (1954) contributes a chapter to *Freud as We Knew Him* that describes Freud's treatment of H.D. (the poet Hilda Doolittle). The H.D. analysis began in 1933, when Freud was 77 and ill. He saw H.D. five to six times per week for a hundred hours, and then for a five-week course some months later. Freud seemed at least as interested in educating H.D. as in curing her; he considered her to be one of many "intellectually special people." He seemed to want to give her a "feel for psychoanalytic ideas and methods"; but he certainly did not seem to care to demonstrate to her analytic technique as he himself defined it. He rode roughshod over boundaries: he had tea with the patient and her family, gave H.D. boughs from his orange tree, and took her on a tour of his collection of antiquities. And he lost his temper with her. It began with a reproach to her for looking at her watch. "You need not keep looking at the time as if you were in a hurry to get away. The trouble is," he says, "I am an old man. You do not think it worth your while to love me."

H.D. writes in her account *Tribute to Freud* (Doolittle 1984), "There was an argument implicit in our very bones." No wonder she reported that on at least one occasion she felt with Freud "like a child summoned to my father's study or my mother's sewing room or told by a teacher to wait in after school." In the face of all this, it is understandable that she ended up seeing "psychoanalysis as a special form of Socratic method, and Socratic method in turn as a kind of fencing." She reports that Freud, in the transference, had acquired both "phallic power and the power to cut." She certainly could have felt cut and perhaps powerless when she rushed to Vienna to commiserate with Freud after one of his patients was killed in a plane crash. Freud repaid her apparent kindness with an interpretation: she was expressing her wish to take the dead patient's place.

This account of so-called analysis does not present a pretty picture. But as always with Freud and technique, puzzle, ambiguity, and contradiction preclude our absolute judgment. If the relationship was only made up of "fencing" and arguing, how does one understand the gloriously poetic tribute to Freud's ability to transform by his words "the grey web . . . dyed blue or scarlet"? How does one incorporate into what appears to be a clinical disaster H.D.'s report that "Many of his words did, in a sense explode . . . opening up mines of hidden treasures"? Even her account of Freud's loss of temper suggests his evocative power: "It was as if the Supreme Being had hammered with his fist on the back of the couch . . . like a child hammering a porridge-spoon on the table."

Perhaps we can presume that despite Freud's technically and emotionally questionable behavior, positive transference asserted itself and colored her report of the interaction. Or perhaps what H.D. experienced with Freud wasn't transference in the transference neurosis sense, but just a general response to his charisma, which struck patients and non-patients alike. Perhaps Freud had remarkable powers of evocativeness that were largely unreported. After all, those involved in psychotherapy in Freud's time were even less aware of the concept of evocativeness—particularly as a way of assessing interventions—than we are.

Perhaps Freud's tone of voice and rhythm of speech and facial expression would, if we had them before us, help clarify these questions. As it is, we can only speculate, as H.D. does, about Freud's state of mind. Holland (1954) tells us that "At the first of their sessions, H.D., instead of saying something, looks at his antiquities. She reports, 'What he said—I thought a little sadly—was, "You are the only person who has ever come into this room and looked at the things in the room before looking at me."'" With that remark, Freud might have led H.D. to recognize that everything that she did and said was worth noting—implying, as he did so, that each of her actions had meaning. He either evoked sadness in her, or he was sad. Either way, he helped her to begin to be aware that she used intellectual-aesthetic interests to avoid such feelings as sadness, and to avoid, too, the presumed anxiety of speaking at the beginning of this, their first, meeting.

Although Freud's patients supply some details about his charisma and evocative power, what one misses in his case reports is a sense of the whole person. Instead, we mainly get descriptions of dynamics, conflicts, and events. Freud rarely uses his vaunted literary skills to create evocative images for the reader. True to his exploratory task, he offers a record of his pursuits while giving back little more than reports of theoretical discoveries. Perhaps he was more evocative with his patients than he was in his writing about them. He may have set for himself in his writing a scientific task, one in which, at that time and place, could not include evocativeness. Evocativeness would be viewed as art, and Freud himself would have viewed it as the kind of humanistic indulgence from which he, in his role of hard scientist, was trying to escape.

So ends the case material of Freud and the data that afford us the opportunity to assess his clinical work, especially with respect to evocativeness. Many critics and clinicians have given Freud's clinical writing high marks. Jones, in writing of Freud's report of the Wolf Man's treatment, sees him

> at the very height of his powers a confident master of his method, and the technique he displays in the interpretation and synthesis of the incredibly complex material must win every reader's admiration. Only those who have tried can appreciate how difficult it is to present a long analysis in a coherent and interesting fashion. Few other analysts have succeeded in holding their reader's attention for more than the first pages. Here Freud's unusual literary powers and his capacity for coordinating masses of facts made him easily supreme.

Mahoney cites a prominent attitude toward this material this way:

> A well-presented and engaging case history requires an analyst with scriptive talents, and Freud had them to an unsurpassed degree. His classic cases manifest a blending of associative and critical processes that transmits a flavor of the clinical situation; an empathic quality in object relationships; . . . a powerful rhetorical interweaving of clinician, author, patient, and reader; a theoretical and expository sensitivity to language; and an ability to shift easily and quickly among many frames of reference.

According to Mahoney, Freud's case reports, whether because of their intrinsic worth and persuasiveness, their historical significance, or mere curiosity, "were at the center of most psychoanalytic teaching programs until the 1970's and remain so in many places today. If Freud's works traditionally constituted the basic canon of psychoanalysis, his five case histories were its Pentateuch, its Torah, its canon within the canon."

I can't say that I fully share such enthusiasms, but I do know that for many reasons whatever views one has about Freud are likely to be weighted by the cross of his greatness. Objectivity is hard to come by. All one can hope for is some measure of self-awareness that can put his work in personal perspective. For me, that awareness takes the form of recalling an event. I own a 45 rpm recording of Freud giving a brief message in English. I remember, when I first got the recording, my anticipation of being, however distantly and electronically, in the presence of the great. Freud was speaking a language foreign to him, with a prosthesis in his mouth; he was ill, elderly, probably bored and impatient with new-fangled machinery. Never mind all that: I was disappointed, as so often happens when errant idealization crashes against reality. Cannons didn't go off as they should have. For me he should have come through the thicket of these extraneous difficulties with an evocativeness worthy of a Roosevelt or a Churchill. Instead I heard an unevocative, somewhat querulous-sounding old man.

Yet it is Freud's very greatness, of course, that stirs in people—like me at that time—great expectations and idealizations, and therefore keeps him in the dangerous terrain of imminently disappointing his followers or instilling in them rage and envy. Allowances need to be made for the influence these feelings may have on one's critical views.

For me, Freud's case reports are less a description of a person than they are a collection of pathologies and how they got that way.

Peter Gay (1988) agrees. "These classic clinical reports may appear more impassive or didactic than as clinical performances." I find it somewhat difficult to remember these patients, much as I find it difficult to remember an unevocative film or play.

The limpness of their effect on me is partially understandable since these treatments were in conformity with Freud's major purpose of using his clinical work to confirm and extend his theories. ("Studies" or "investigations" are probably more apt as labels for what occurred than "treatments.") I, on the other hand, was and am primarily interested in both the human interactions and the techniques of defense and character analysis, the role of ego functions, and above all the piquancy inherent in every person and interaction between persons. For this purpose, Freud evidently put aside his humanistic, empathic, evocative sensibilities and such impulses as are revealed in his noting that exchanges with patients were "comparable to the work of novelists" and that great novelists and playwrights were keen psychologists. Schafer (1992) puts it this way with regard to the humanistic-existential aspect of Freud's creations (which implicitly include evocativeness): "Freud could not have been prepared to consider that aspect suitable for theoretical purposes. Instead, he simply took it for granted as a component of both clinical empathy and novelistic feel for the language of clinical work."

Understandable as it is, we can still regret that Freud took that aspect for granted. If he had chosen to take it more seriously, he could have created imagery far different from that of the mirror and surgeon, images that he inadvertently fastened onto the imagination of generations of therapists as characteristic of psychoanalytic technique. He could have saved himself and the rest of us a lot of trouble had he written systematically about the intimacies and nuances of the relationship between therapist and patient. He could have thwarted those often politically motivated revisionist claims that "classical" psychoanalysts are emotionally cold and solipsistically one-person. And he might have influenced the ways that therapists express themselves, in words and print. He might have prevented such assessments as that of Schafer (1992), who notes "the drab style of much of psychoanalytic literature," and Kanzer and Glenn (1980) who describe "the lackluster writing we find today in all but a few psychoanalysts' articles." Mahoney (1996) affirms these dour observations, and ties his affirmation specifically to the lack of that quality of empathy that would allow for identification. Despite the recognition and emphasis on this process in clinical teaching and practice, "the absence of internalizability characterizes much psychoanalytic prose today . . . insofar as much writing in contemporary psychoanalytic journals and books is insipid, it tends to be noninternalizable. The medium undercuts the message when impersonal prose is used to promote internalization." Where was Freud (in this respect) when we needed him?

Freud was less than enthusiastic about the therapeutic results of analysis. In a letter to Fliess in 1897 he complained of "continual disappointments in my attempts [at] bringing my analysis to a real conclusion, the running away of people who had for a time seemed almost in my grasp, the absence of the complete successes on which I had reckoned, the possibility of explaining the partial successes in other ways. . . ." That assessment was not just the result of the abreactive-cathartic model that he was using at the time, or of his inexperience. His final summation on the subject, in 1937, was also on the whole pessimistic.

In "Analysis Terminable and Interminable," Freud (1937) ascribed the limitations of analytic effectiveness to many causes, notably biological and physical ones (adhesiveness of the libido) and to such death instinct derivatives as the negative therapeutic reaction, the repetition compulsion, and the intensity of resistances. Neither here nor elsewhere does he vigorously focus upon the person of the therapist, or the therapist's selection, training, and personality, to say nothing of the microscopic detail of evocative interventions. The effect of one person on another, if attended to at all, was conveyed in stark terms of transference and countertransference.

The above-quoted Fliess letter offers nonclinical data to support Freud's sometime lack of evocativeness. Take, for example, the imagery inherent in his characterization of patients who had not been loyal to the treatment: ". . . the running away of people who had for a time seemed almost in my grasp." Conceiving of a patient as "running away" and being or not being "grasped" is hardly the way to encourage a therapeutic alliance, an "atmosphere of safety" (Schafer 1983) or to encourage one to join in the frightening inner world that could be evoked if each party were free to do so. This grasping, rather than holding, this pursuer and pursued conception is consonant with the pre-psychoanalytic model of the tasks of the therapist as consisting primarily of chasing and finding the traumatic event that was causing the symptom. Freud tells us nothing explicitly, nor much implicitly either, of his changing his way of working with patients. And in fact he probably was inclined to continue his original ways if, as Ellman (1991) and others aver, he continued through his life to be influenced by the traumatic event conception. He continued to "pursue" and "grasp" instead of encouraging self-discovery by flying on the wings of evoked feeling and thought.

9

At Work with Evocativeness— Case Examples

In Part II of this book, I illustrate with clinical material both successfully evocative interventions and those that can be improved upon. The case material was collected adventitiously, from the work of supervisors, friends, and colleagues, and sometimes it is made up. All of the material is disguised. The material was not easy to get. Promised material was not delivered or delayed, and I found in myself resistance to imagined criticisms and embarrassing exposure of my clinical thinking. No wonder psychoanalysis is heavy with speculation, light with data.

The method of presentation is—with some exceptions—to put the usually verbatim data in the left-hand column of the page, with my comments, from the standpoint of evocativeness, in the right-hand facing column.

At times I quote exactly what I would have said in the clinical situation. At other times I include multiple ideas in a single intervention, thereby seeming to talk at greater length than I customarily would.

So let us now enter those golden moments of opportunity for two souls to come together evocatively.

FLOWER SHOW

The therapist reported telling a patient that "she seemed like a flower poking its head up through a crack in the sidewalk only to be squashed." He preceded his recounting of the intervention to me with the apology that what he was about to say was corny, and he wished he had not said it. When asked why he was apologetic about his remark, he repeated that it was "corny . . . the sort of thing one encounters on greeting cards." The patient, however, responded with evident appreciation, saying that she did feel that her little efforts had often been squashed. (1)

(1) Here we have an instance of the therapist being evocative despite himself, disavowing the feelings evoked in himself that gave rise to the evocative remark. What was rejected by him as "corny" was experienced by the patient as a relief from a lifetime of being misunderstood in a family whose members had all graduated from prestigious, strongly academic, and definitely not corny schools. She had had far too much sophistication and intellectualization in the past, which had squashed her flower self. To her, a corny greeting card, no matter the occasion, was a valentine.

The therapist's apparent discomfort at the feeling engendered by the thought that led to the intervention may have been responsible for his mildly unfortunate choice of "poking," a vigorous, "phallic-intrusive" word that would not capture her experience as well as the gentler "pushing" or still better, "raising" or "lifting." Such words reflect the patient's worried-hopeful attempt at newness, like a baby's exploration, a basically oral inner atmosphere. Alternatively, her experience could have primarily been one of forcing against resistance, and so the entering, struggling imagery would be accurate. This is an example of how useful it is to gauge correctly the psychosexual mode in which the patient is operating at a particular moment. By recognizing the mode and insinuating one's self into its atmosphere the therapist is more likely to find the words that best fit the occasion.

WILD ANALYSIS

The story is all too familiar The
patient is intellectually brilliant,
physically beautiful, and intuitively sensitive to the nuances
of human nature. But instead of
pursuing a style of life commen-
surate with her gifts, she
dropped out of college and married a manual worker, beneath
her in everything that mattered
to her. She threw herself into
the roles of wife and mother
with her accustomed skill and
drive, squeezing every bit of
personal satisfaction from her
effort. As with everything she
had undertaken she performed
well. Predictably, it was not
enough. She described to the

therapist how odd, apart, ill-
fitting she felt, how miserable
she was in the geographical and
social world to which she
seemed condemned. After the
patient described a frighteningly
boring evening in the company
of her husband and his friends
(merely her acquaintances) the
therapist commented, "You
make it sound like a concentration camp." The therapist offered as a rationale for her
comment the intention of empathizing and sympathizing with
the plight of the patient. But the
patient at first fell silent, then
said she felt criticized. (1)

(1) Well-meaning as the therapist may have been, her choice
of intervention ended by being
unevocative at best, and stifling
of evocativeness at worst. To
begin with, the therapist made
no attempt to find out what
aspects of concentration camps
were resonant with the patient.
Was it the lack of opportunity
to get out? Was it her tortured
experience of daily life? Did the
patient interpret her poor fit
with others as proof of her bad-

ness, and so make her imprison-
ment deserved? These hardly
exhaust the possibilities. The
therapist would have had a better chance of being evocative
had she invited more of the patient's thoughts about the awful
evening. The therapist could
have then intervened in a way
that jibed with what was most
emotionally meaningful to the
patient. Instead, she practiced, in
effect, "wild analysis," assuming
without exploring.

Not getting the relevant information about the patient's
understanding and feelings at the
moment resulted in the therapist's intervention being heard as
critical, and as similar to the
patient's mother accusing her of
dramatizing her various plights
in order to extract sympathy.
The sequence was: patient's
description, therapist's association to concentration camp, and
therapist's telling that association
to the patient. The sequence
should have been: patient's description, therapist's association
to concentration camp, then the
therapist's turning over in her

mind possible meanings to the patient of the concentration camp experience, inviting more details about the torturous evening in order to see whether any of the concentration camp meanings reverberated with the patient's experience. If, for example, the most convincing evidence pointed to the patient feeling trapped in unremitting misery, the therapist might have said something like, "Your description of that evening made me shudder; it is as if you felt yourself in a concentration camp, unable to escape and facing the death of all you hold dear." The therapist might then have been able to helpfully examine the patient's experience, founded on the unexamined assumptions, that there was, in fact, nothing she could do about her plight. She might have then moved toward the realization that she herself was her jailer, the executioner of ingenuity and hope.

REAL ESTATE

(P. had just moved into a new apartment.)

P: Yeah, my parents said to buy whatever I need . . . but I want to keep the costs down, so I've really kept to a strict budget. I have a bed, but no furniture. I bought the cheapest stupid little pan I could find, and one fork, one knife, one spoon, and one plate. I will even buy the cheapest spaghetti sauce that tastes bad, but I like it.

T: It sounds like you are a prisoner in your own apartment. (1)

(1) The prisoner image is potentially evocative, but its power is lost since it fails to pick up where the patient seems to be at the moment. She is imprisoned by some ideas that she has, but the intervention shades more toward external servitude.

P: Yeah, well, I'm trying to save money—because even though they say to buy whatever I need, they will complain when they actually get the bill . . . so I only shop at Walmart, K-Mart, and Price Choppers. (2)

(2) It is likely that the patient left out of her recounting expressions of feelings of injustice, deprivation, anger, and perhaps disappointment in the parents' hypocrisy. These may have been covered in the therapy previously, but if not already thoroughly worked on and through, they should be here. After all, the patient is on the spot. At some level she likely would prefer better living arrangements, and she has been invited to have them, but she doesn't trust the invitation. Perhaps one could

evoke that feeling of frustration and unsureness about how she should proceed.

T: We have talked before about how you feel your parents have mistreated you, but today I get the idea that there are certain ways you disapprove of yourself. (3)

(3) This comment raises the question of whether the patient's self-deprivation is the result of fear of the parents' disapproval, and of ultimately feeling rejection, and perhaps shame over greed, or whether her remark stems from an introjection of the parents, a self-deprivation by way of identifying with them, becoming like them with respect to their treatment of her. The next step toward answering that subtle question would be to evoke the feelings at the moment. The patient should be exploring verbally the markers between, in effect, projective and introjective stances.

P: Well, you have to push yourself to get ahead. For example, I'd like to be a writer, and so I've written

eight paragraphs every day
since 1991—and my writing
has improved . . . or at
least I think it has—so it's
really the only way to do
it—to push yourself . . .
Every day, whether you feel
like it or not, I make myself
write those eight paragraphs.
I think all the great writers
are probably familiar with
what I'm talking about. It's
not easy to be a writer. (4)

(4) The patient seems to be answering the question we posed.
However much she may dread
and fear the parents' reaction to
her spending their money, she
has built into herself not only
the need but at least the quasi-
pleasure of working hard, involving a deprivation that she
sees as appropriate and as fitting
in with her longer-range goals.
Alongside the anger and disappointment and distrust, she
likely has feelings of satisfaction,
even perhaps a kind of closeness
to her parents from adhering to
what she takes to be their values.
This experience may lie emo-

tionally a layer beneath the hostility, but maybe not.

One could invite her to reflect on how important is it to her to set up and stick with such a writing schedule and what feelings and thoughts she has when contemplating doing it, when doing it, and when she is finished.

T: I was just thinking production assembly lines, and how hard it is to leave time to be creative when you are under the pressure to produce. (5)

(5) T. introduces his own fantasy here which implies that the patient is suffering the noncreative boredom and routinization of factory assembly lines. That does not seem to be the way the patient experiences her writing regime. It would have been better to invite the patient to say more about her self-imposed routine, her experience of it, how it fits or doesn't fit with the style and needs of each parent for her. She might uncover positively toned experiences around work or around pleasing the parents apart from submitting

out of fear. And, incidentally, T's comments imply that the patient is, under the present circumstances, uncreative. She could easily hear that as criticism and demandingness instead of the empathy which T perhaps intended in making the remark.

P: I love assembly lines! Like in Dr. Seuss's books—all of those whimsical little assembly lines! (6)

(6) The patient pretty clearly sets T. straight about introducing her own fantasy and/or being unempathetically out of attunement. Metaphorically, the patient could be saying that she finds something loving and fun in her self-imposed regime, as we speculated.

The moral of the story for the analyst here is to be careful of introducing his own ideas and images (the prisoner, assembly lines) without first being reasonably sure that he is extending and evoking correctly the patient's as yet insufficiently expressed thoughts and feelings, and without assessing whether he is attuned to the patient's concerns.

IMPULSE BUYING

T: . . . under which you hid
your secret impulsivity. (1)

(1) "You hid your secret" can
easily be heard as criticism, especially when it is linked with a
word like "impulsivity." Impulsivity is a cold, technical term
likely evocative of nothing more
than affront. Worse, it proceeds
from a model of people *having*
pathological things, an unfortunate borrowing from the disease
model of physical medicine.
Real life is not composed of
such discrete personality units.
Rather, if one wants to use the
term at all, it should be cast in
terms of behavior, for example,
"at times you make decisions

and act without giving yourself
the benefit of considering the
consequences. At those times
you probably feel that you have
to act, to get what you feel you
need regardless of the consequences."

FAMILY MATTERS

The family of the hospitalized
patient lives in the same city,
but hardly ever visits, or even
contacts the patient in other
ways. This behavior is consistent
with the way family members
have always acted toward her.
The patient shows the same
blandness as other family members. She is more inclined to
threaten and attempt suicide,
acting more than confronting
her feelings and opinions, especially about the family's style of
interaction.

T: You need the support of
your family. (1)

(1) Support comes in many shapes, sizes, and guises and the word is so easily overused. To rescue support's experiential meaning to this patient from its potential for generality and dullness, one might say to her, "You don't much show it, maybe aren't even aware of it, but somewhere in you is a lost, lonely, abandoned child crying out for somebody or something that she can depend on, can call her own."

PRODUCTION AND REPRODUCTION

This unmarried woman has
been labeled as having one or
another variety of schizophrenia
for many years as she has gone
in and out of one or another
hospital program. Her therapist
had left for a week, thus necessi-
tating the cancellation of one
meeting. During the week of
the missed meeting, the patient
developed paranoid and somatic
delusions. An example of the
latter is that she believed she
could not evacuate or urinate
and that, as a result, ultimately,
she would explode.

T: I think you've developed
these ideas and symptoms as

a way of making sure I'll
come back. (1)

(1) The therapist has the right
idea, and expresses it succinctly.
However, his intervention is a
shade pallid and intellectual-
sounding. He could have said,
for example, "You must have
been worried that I wouldn't
come back. It's hard for you to
believe that I am dependably
with you unless you force me to
be—by appearing to be sick and
needful. You seem to find it
hard to meet me with words, to
talk with me person-to-person,
so you let your body do the
talking. You could have saved
yourself a lot of trouble by simply telling me with words to be
sure to come back, that you feel
better when you're with me,
that you need us to work together.

"As to holding on to your
feces and urine, that tells me
that you desperately fear losing
yourself if you lose me. You
probably feel desperate to hold
on to everything you have.
Having things that you own
with you must give you a feel-

ing of being a secure self, solid and safe."

T. and P. make plans to resume their meetings, in the course of which the therapist tells the patient that he will be available to continue working with her all through the next year. Shortly after that she tells hospital personnel that she is pregnant. She can tell because she sees herself as fat in the abdomen.

T: You have a new symptom. (He thinks but does not say to the patient that she had eroticized their intention to resume meetings.) (2)

(2) The therapist is probably well-advised not to articulate the heterosexual theme, as if the patient were in an hysterical oedipal mode. Instead, the therapist repeats his previous intervention about her using her body to present a symptom that will help guarantee "medical attention." Another possibility could be that she experienced their resuming meetings as an opportunity for new life, growth, flowering; in short,

hope. This idea and more importantly her feeling about herself as "pregnant" needs to be supported and implemented—as it could be were the therapist to say, "I think our resuming meetings, our getting together, has produced a feeling of a new life being possible for you. That's a wonderful idea. Once again, when you trust and believe in words, you'll be less likely to use your body; then you can be pregnant with our relationship and work together with hope for the developing future."

Introducing "pregnancy" in the therapist–patient dialogue, especially with a quasi-delusional patient is not without risk. Sometimes high risk comes with high gain.

AN OPENING

After years of occupational and marital failure that the patient regularly explained as being due to external circumstances, he offered the following:

P: Maybe there's something in me that makes it difficult to keep jobs.

T: Why might *that* be?

(The patient drops the subject into a cloud of obsessional verbiage.) (1)

(1) The therapist is right to move in on the crack in the patient's longtime externalizing defense and try to take advan-

tage of the patient's apparent insight. But she doesn't seem to sense the full implications of his statement, or at any rate doesn't pursue them energetically. She could have taken advantage of several opportunities for evocativeness, such as: the importance for their work together of internalizing rather than externalizing; the gravity of the existential situation; an intense curiosity about his unconscious motives; insinuations about the feelings and fantasies that are responsible for the patient's self-defeating acts and why he has externalized the responsibility for them so tenaciously.

Instead of "Why might that be?" suppose for example that the therapist had responded along these lines: "Oh my! Let's look closer at what you've just said. You seem to be considering that while a part of you struggles manfully to work and get ahead, another part of you has all along been sabotaging your efforts. If that's true, there are *no* jobs or wives that you will allow to be successful. What

a terrible spot to be in—
working so hard both for and
against yourself. And time goes
by. You must have imagined
something awful would happen
if you did allow success. Locat-
ing the source of your difficulty
in yourself gives us the chance
to explore those awful imaginings, and put them in their
place."

I at first wrote, about the fantasies in the last sentence,
". . . to put them to rest." I
then speculated that such oral
imagery as "put to rest" was not
likely to resonate helpfully with
this man at this moment. While
he was all too prone to one or
another variety of passivity and
wishful thinking, right now he
was noticing and beginning to
explore the phallic side of himself. "To put them in their
place" with its call to action, a
slight touch of roughness, and a
suggestion of mastery, is where
we want to be.

ARE YOU REALLY THERE?

P: Then sometimes I worry if you daydream when I'm talking. I'm sure you do sometimes because it's a really human thing.

T: I wonder if this is related to your feeling with Ben [which she had just been talking about]. You're talking about something important, and you worry that I'm not there with you. (1)

(1) The therapist could have chosen to do a bit of defense analysis here, taking up the patient's volunteering excuses for the therapist just after implicitly accusing the therapist of inatten-

tion. That analysis of the defense
might have helped to get to the
emotions inherent in her
accusation—for example, feeling abandoned, unimportant,
boring, or closeted with a person who thinks she has more
important things to think about.
But instead of analyzing that
self-defeating defense, the therapist shifts the implicit emotions
directed toward her to someone
else: Ben. Even that could have
been turned to evocative advantage if the therapist had that task
in mind. But instead of exploring the emotions with regard to
Ben she leaves the statement at
the level of one thing being "related" to another.

The use of the abstract, inexplicit "related" is perhaps a clue
to an emotional withdrawal
from the patient to which the
patient might be reacting in
bringing up the daydream accusation. Presumably the patient
has some powerful feelings
about others' inattention to her.
These could be fruitfully evoked
if the therapist is willing to get
into them with the patient.

Calling some topic or session "important" carries the possibility of further stimulating interest in what has been discussed, and so could aid in evocativeness. It is, however, dangerous in that it implies (at least to the unconscious) that other discussions and topics and sessions are not considered important. Moreover, it puts the therapist in a judging role, which detracts from the feeling of safety so necessary for the patient's being able to speak freely. The advantages could be secured with less danger if one were to say, "important *to you*."

As to suggesting that the patient is "worried" about the therapist's supposed inattention, the therapist's choosing to limit it to "worry" works against evoking the hotter emotions that might be blazing—maybe not only worry but rage, humiliation, hurt feelings. Even if worry was the dominant feeling it would be helpfully evocative to learn whether that worry was more like a wisp of an idea that crossed the patient's mind, or a conviction that the therapist's attention is undependable.

The phrase "there with you" may once have been helpfully evocative, for example, encouraging the safety of an alliance, or offering a sense of a dependable ally, among other possibilities. It is difficult not to be tempted by the possible evocative gain of such imagery. But the phrase has now been swept up into New Age jargon and is therefore subject to dismissal if the patient eschews that jargon. Along with the patient's dismissal of the language and whatever ideas it may refer to here, the therapist may also be dismissed as a linguistic lightweight. It could have been worse. The therapist could have chosen the even more jargony "not there for you." "With you" at least has the advantage of evoking the feeling of an alliance.

THE FIGHT AGAINST FIGHTING

The patient has attempted suicide numerous times, and regularly threatens to do it
successfully. In other respects,
she is characterized by the therapist and hospital staff as inordi-
nately "passive," and she refers
to herself that way also.

T: We need to find out the
purpose of your passivity. (1)

(1) Here is a suggested alterna-
tive: "Passive? You have half the
hospital in fits thinking what to
do with you, jumping when the
telephone rings, fearing for your
life. Some passivity! You're one
of the most active people in this
place."

The patient briefly looks irritated.

T: You seem to me to be angry.
(2)

> (2) To begin with, the phraseology is tentative—"seem" and "to me." A "passive" patient might require more vigor from the therapist. "Angry" is overused, and has lost much of its ability to grab one's attention. An alternative might be: "You look mad as hell. You've got fire blazing in your eyes. You should see it—get a mirror sometime and look."

The patient opens her eyes a bit wider, showing a spark, shifts in her chair, then sinks back into her accustomed slouch. The therapist's response to this (acknowledged to her supervisor) is hopelessness. The therapist reports that the patient just doesn't get engaged. She says she doesn't know what to do with the patient at this point. This is what she does do.

T: You turn away from me, your best chance to get better. (3)

(3) The disconsolate therapist also turns away, from the patient. She tries to counteract that recognition through the use of "get better." That cliché, borrowed from professional and colloquial overuse, is banal and uninspiring. She could have said, "You turn away from me, your best chance to get somewhere else in life," or "to get back your old-time zest and enthusiasm," or "to learn to live again."

In reference to the patient shifting in her chair, "Just then you allowed yourself a fleeting sample of rage. Then something happened! You gave it up, just as you gave up a chance to express yourself, to know yourself, maybe enjoy yourself. You felt a stirring in your gut, a sample of rage, and scared yourself half to death. Somewhere you must be terrified at what you *imagine* would happen if you were to tell me, or the world—or yourself—how much you sometimes would like to destroy us."

P: I'm damaged.

T: That's how you're looking at it *now*. (4)

(4) The therapist is right in calling attention to the patient's loss of time perspective, a common feature in the suicidal experience. The comment often is quite helpful in reorienting patients toward a more realistic appraisal of themselves and their circumstances. In this instance, however, there is something even more promising to work with at the moment—the patient's claim of damage.

For example: "I don't know what damage you're talking about, but the one that I see is cowardice. Everybody's damaged, one way or another. The difference is how a person deals with it. I called you a coward because you run from life's challenges, you take refuge in withdrawal, you excuse yourself, you claim hopeless damage. Yes, loss of nerve goes on the top of your list of damages. In plain English, that's "cowardice."

This kind of intervention is

designed to shake up the system.
It challenges the patient with its
slightly insulting name-calling,
and it dissociates the interaction
from psychobabble and do-
goodism; this veteran patient has
heard all of that before. Now
the usual clinical clichés and
empty reassurances would either
garner her contempt or stir up
guilt and self-devaluation at all
these nice people trying to be
helpful in the face of her intran-
sigence.

LOVE TERROR

Throughout a decade of treatment the patient has been labeled a schizophrenic. She
missed many of her first individual therapy sessions with a
new therapist. He was less than
vigorous in reacting to these
absences out of a fear that he
would upset her. In doing so, he
was, he said, doing supportive
psychotherapy. The therapist's
supervisor asked him to consider
the possibility that she was testing him—Did he care whether
she came or not? Did he want
her as a patient in the first place?
In the sessions she sat hunched
over and averted her eyes. Just
once she turned briefly to look

at the therapist before resuming
her customary bodily avoidance.

T: (Silence.) (1)

(1) What the patient doesn't
need is silence. For this patient
at this time, the emptiness of
silence is an invitation to entertain primary process fantasies.
Unchecked by reality, these
shield her from interaction with
what is to her a fearsome world,
the agent of which is her new
therapist. Deficient in dependable ego functioning, she needs
to borrow his. He needs to per-
form for her those functions that
she chooses not to exercise
herself—to check with reality,
to take initiative, to exercise
judgment, to guide interactions
with others, to anchor her. All
of this could be conveyed more
or less directly to the patient.
Paradoxically, the very directness that the therapist fears
would be upsetting would, if
done with tact, timing, and in
an evocative manner, be supportive—or, as in the aphorism,
"sometimes the most supportive
intervention is an interpreta-

tion." The task here is to convey to the patient the therapist's willingness, even verve, to be *with* the patient, to be a strong, palpable presence. This would be done not necessarily with verbal assurance, which at best would most likely be disbelieved, and at worst could be resented as infantilizing. (It's likely she has heard such superficial reassurances many times in her previous years of treatment.) The therapist needs to make contact with that part of her that *did* attend five meetings, and that was encapsulated in her momentary making of eye contact.

One might, for example, say something like, "I notice that you usually turn away from looking at me. That tells me how terrified you are at being with me. So naturally you decided to stay away from some of our meetings and to keep your thoughts to yourself. How courageous you were to allow yourself that quick look at me. I hope you found what you are looking for, someone to really be with you."

THE PAST NOT TAKEN

In incident after incident the patient portrays himself as constantly miserable, a tragic figure.

P: I must be masochistic.

T: What do you mean? How are you using that word? (1)

> (1) Jargon and labels are unlikely to be evocative, and they often obscure the meanings embedded in them. The therapist is right to ask what the patient means.

P: Well, sort of I mean enjoying pain, making sure things turn out bad, always the loser.

T: What are your thoughts and feelings about that as applied to yourself?

P: (Figuratively kicking the therapist in the shins.) Same old, same old.

T: Yes, very old; we know you were unhappy in your family. Remember those scenes where father beat up your brother, and you hid under the bed, afraid that you'd get it next?

P: Yes, I know I keep repeating the past. It's a bad deal.

He sighs resignedly, then is silent, as if waiting for the therapist to take over. His voice and demeanor are affectively flat. He appears not to be interested and assumes the therapist feels the same way. (2)

(2) The therapist responds somewhat defensively to the patient's dig. It would have been better to take up and evoke the patient's anger and/or fear, which likely underlie what he means by "masochistic." Here, the heat of the moment between the therapist and patient is lost when the therapist

moves to the past, however correct the formulation may be.

When one takes up an issue can be at times just as useful and evocative as *how* one takes it up.

The patient has at least a rudimentary knowledge of how he behaves, even sometimes of the roots of his behavior. The technical problem is for him to allow the implications of the paths he chooses to get past his defensive barriers, and for him to allow himself to have feelings and perspective. He needs not only to be expressive—to get things off his chest, to re-enact the past with new awareness and perspective (helpful, indeed necessary as these might be at the right time)—but to *care!* The therapist could have said, "You sound to me uninvolved, even bored, yet you're telling me that you are resigned to being a miserable loser for *the rest of your life.*" The therapist speaks quietly but forcefully, with twinges of horror and sadness at the wasted life whose grim outlines are pushing insistently into their awareness. The therapist uses the tone one might hear around a deathbed. He looks steadily, unwaveringly at the patient's eyes as he speaks. His evenness and deliberateness—just a slight pause between words— foreshadows the underlying shriek.

The therapist could continue by asking if the patient wants to remain at a distance from himself, let the past repeat itself. Is he the director, as well as the lead actor, in this play? Or, the therapist asks, do *we* push past resignation and pursue a different path, no longer to be "masochistic"? In so doing, the therapist models, demonstrates, and lends the experience of self that the patient yearns for but at the same time has been trying to ward off. The therapist tries in these ways to evoke the existential perspective that the patient needs in order to inspire efforts to change.

WORKING THE VINEYARD

The patient has a long history of
alcoholism, and of rage to the
point of homicidal inclinations.
He repeatedly takes more medicine than his doctor prescribes.
He explains this behavior
vaguely as being necessitated by
his bodily symptoms, or lamely
as his having figured out that if a
little helps, then more will help
even more.

    The therapist could have tried
to educate the patient as to the
dangers of not following the
prescribed routine, along the
way reminding him of his invet-
erate breaking of rules. Instead,
the therapist took it as her task
to get to the more salient and

largely unconscious reasons for
his behavior. Taking into consideration his decades of alcoholism, his apparently ungiving
parents, and his fury on a level
inappropriate to situations, she
said, "I think I can understand
why you take more than your
prescription calls for. You have
suffered all your life from a feeling of never having gotten
enough—of anything. At those
moments of deprivation, when
you are deciding to increase
your dosage, you feel in your
stomach a great emptiness
(therapist makes a circular mo-
tion around her stomach area).
That emptiness is accompanied
by deep despair that things will
ever be different—and by rage
at the constantly depriving
world. Whether it's your doctor's skimpy dosage of medicine,
your girlfriend's not attending to
you as much as you crave, or
my ending our too few sessions,
the feeling is the same—
emptiness and hunger, rage and
despair. We need to fill that
emptiness, to fill that hunger,
and cool that rage." (1)

(1) However consciously rea-
soned or simply intuitive, in
choosing an intervention the
therapist was guided by diagnostic understanding. She placed
the patient in an oral-
dependent, oral-aggressive,
primitively organized level of
psychosexual understanding, and
proceeded accordingly. She
might have been tempted by her
own needs to take an educative
approach, but decided against it;
surely, through the years the
patient had heard more than
enough of the supposed advantages of following the rules. He
would also not benefit from
once again hearing about the
effects on others of his behavior;
he was too imbued with his
own needs to care about that.
Instead of serving as a motivator,
such an intervention, perhaps
seen as taking the part of others,
would not only be experienced
by him as a desertion of neutrality, but as a stimulus to nonpro-
ductive guilt and resentment.

The therapist offers instead an
interpretation. She begins it
with "I think." Some patients

would find this construction welcoming, contributing to an atmosphere of reflectiveness, the sort of thoughtfulness that can be inserted between urges and actions that would be ideal for a person given to impulsively giving in to desires and actions. Other patients would hear "I think" as indecisive and weak, and tend to dismiss whatever came after the "I think."

The gist of her intervention is forceful. She asserts, in effect, that the patient is motivated by orality and its derivatives. But she frames that assertion in a nice blend of kindness and empathy. She is emotionally with the patient in his experience of temptation and drivenness. When she makes circular motions near her stomach with her hand, she "talks" the primitive language of the body, and picks the area where his yearnings are likely located. By using such language as "all your life" and "constantly" she implicitly reminds the patient that she and he are talking not only about an incident but of a lifelong pattern with all of the intimations of happiness and tragedy of that perspective.

She ends with a call for joint action on the patient's behalf, with a clarifying statement of their task, and a subtle but inspiring promise that together they can be successful. All in all, she has delivered her message evocatively.

THE PRISONERS

This male patient in his twenties
is in jail for stealing cars. Having
tested Superior by the prison
psychologist, he was thought to
be a good candidate for "counseling." However, he literally
refused to talk except for an
occasional pronouncement ("I
am the smartest person in this
place") and derisive comments
about everybody and everything. He seemed quite comfortable with his refusal to talk.

The therapist offered him the
opportunity for them to get
acquainted, and told him that
unlike the court, she was interested in him rather than his
crime and was not about to

judge his behavior. She suggested that he had reasons for
doing whatever he did, and that
maybe it would be helpful for
now and in the future to know
himself, all the better to have a
better future, and so on. In response, the patient changed his
behavior not a whit. (1)

(1) The therapist did many of
the "right things"; but this patient had heard it all before. Every repetition merely solidified
his devaluing and grandiose rejection of what was being offered him.

Perhaps this would have
helped: "Look Mr. Jones, you
didn't ask to be here, and neither did I. We are both prison-
ers, stuck with one another. The
only question is what are we
going to do about it. Any
ideas?"

What is being evoked here, in
contrast with the more usual
evocation of buried emotional
experience, is a no-nonsense
image, a presence unlike the
patient's stereotyped views of
the "helping profession." He
was confronted with someone

with whom he could, while
saving face, share a similar predicament. And he was as much
in charge of what was to tran-
spire as the putative therapist
was. Thus, he could maintain
his grandiose assuming of the
leadership, controlling role. The
power and self-esteem that he
stole, along with the wheels,
was available to him here for
the taking. That would provide
another kind of vehicle, to be
used for engagement in what
they are doing together.

COLLUSION

This takes place after several
sessions on which T. reports as
follows: "The patient and I have
discussed how she is comfortable
acting out her aggression with
me, but extremely uncomfortable naming or discussing it."

T: Apropos of how uncomfortable acts of aggression are, I
need to tell you that I won't
be working next Monday.
It's a holiday, President's
Day, and I won't be here. (1)

(1) "Apropos" could stir shame
in the patient if she doesn't
know what the foreign term
means, which would set up an
"I'm smarter than you" kind of

relationship. Worse, it sounds apologetic, as if the therapist needs to have some excuse for making her announcement. Perhaps the therapist feels that canceling the session is an "act of aggression." The phrase is also unevocative, jargon, and inexplicit. The apologetic possibility is further supported by the therapist's saying, "I need . . ." as if she is doing something bad to the patient that requires that it be blamed on an external "need."

P: That's okay. Um, so I'll just see you the next Monday.

T: Do you want to set up something before that?

P: What do you have?

T: (lists times throughout the week, and after the holiday.)

P: Maybe Tuesday . . . No, no, I'm going to Des Moines, and that's it. I said I wouldn't go Monday because I was going to come to see you. So I'm gone Tuesday and I'm not changing my plans.

T: Okay. So I'll see you on Monday, February 24, unless I hear from you again.

P: So I have to decide now. I'm not coming.

T: That's fine. But it's okay to call if you need to.

P: Okay. (2)

(2) This material provides an excellent example of how to *prevent* evoking underlying thoughts and feelings and at the same time evoking something undesirable. Instead of employing an expressive-interpretive mode, patient and therapist collude here in establishing and implementing an action mode, which keeps the discussion on the unemotional surface, sealing over what are likely to be painful, if not explosive, feelings.

One way to have gotten to the underlying experience would have been for the therapist simply to announce that she would not be available for such and such a meeting. This would have left the field as a blank page on which the patient could have written her heartfelt story—what it meant to her to be "canceled," especially when she had taken a step toward the therapist by making her plans so that she could meet with the therapist. She may well have felt humiliated, or "learned" once again the lesson not to trust, expose herself, or care. It's likely that she could, in addition, have felt rage at such faithlessness.

At this point the therapist's suggestion that they set up a replacement time rings hollow, and sounds more like another bit of apologetic expiation than a genuine desire to get some more work done together. Worse, from the standpoint of evocativeness, it deprives both of them of the chance to learn what the patient's thoughts and feelings were, not only about the announcement, but about the possibility of replacing the meeting. Why didn't the patient make the suggestion? Was she so traumatized by the "rejection"? Was she already putting in place her ancient decision never to trust, to expose herself, to feel vulnerable? Was she trying to punish the therapist, or at least not give the therapist the satisfaction of letting the therapist feel wanted? The therapist's saying, "That's fine" to the end of the negotiation suggests that what "is fine" is having negotiated this incident without having to deal with the underlying feelings and fantasies.

None of these possibilities come out, however, as they busy themselves with possible meeting dates. Rage, however, does get a quasi-airing in what sounds like truculence or defiance as the patient says "That's it," evidently having lost patience with the whole discussion and its suppressed but still painful stabs. "I'll be going Tuesday, and I'm not changing my plans," she concludes. The therapist could perhaps have opened things up with some such remark as, "I thought I noticed a bit of defiance in your voice. Perhaps we could have a look at that," or "Apart from the planning that we have to do, what thoughts and feelings might you have about this discussion?" Or one might, with some patients, sort of guess that in a situation like that "one could feel disappointment, start thinking one wasn't wanted, maybe get angry." The possibilities, of course, are many, but they are all of no avail so long as there is a collusion between the two not to feel and discuss the existential implications of what might seem a trivial matter of missing or rescheduling one meeting, but that really involves the primal themes of being wanted or not wanted, being abandoned or safe.

THE MISSING MOTHER

The patient gives a number of derivatives pointing in the direction of holding, primitive needfulness, and orality, including the wish to have needs satisfied without having to ask for the satisfaction.

T: Sounds like a child wanting to be held by its mother.

P: I don't want to talk about being held. You make it sound like an accusation, and anyway it's just more Freudian bullshit. (1)

(1) The therapist was on the right track. He had heard and interpreted the derivatives cor-

rectly. His pithy "deep" interpretation could have been, and
perhaps was, evocative. More
likely, however, especially in
view of the patient's reaction, it
missed being maximally evocative, and, as with many interpretations of that kind, carried a
substantial degree of risk. At the
least it provided the patient with
an opportunity to intellectualize
and dismiss the anxiety-
provoking primitive experience.
When the therapist plunges into
the underlying memory, it could
easily be heard by the patient as
accusatory or triumphantly
clever. What the interpretation
did not do was to evoke from
the patient the texture and nuances of the holding experience.
One could, for example, have
mused or questioned or somehow gotten into the experience
of the feeling of arms around
one, of warmth, of softness, of
feeling protected, of "knowing
beyond knowing" that one
would be taken care of even
without asking, perhaps without
one's self knowing what was
hungered for. Was there a

lullaby in the mothering scene?
Perhaps not then or ever, or
perhaps not remembered at the
moment because it was sensed as
too painful—the wish for
sound, the disappointment of
sound's ending, the rage at the
wrong kind of sound.

When I pointed out some of
the ways that the therapist
missed opportunities to be
evocative, the therapist said that
he had translated the image of a
child being held into the experience of his holding his own
child. Probably that was in part
only an attempt to justify his
relative lack of evocativeness
with his patient: the implication
was that the image that was so
moving to him should have
been enough to move the patient. But then the therapist began to fill in with the supervisor
the details of the therapist's own
experience. His voice got softer.
He spoke more slowly and de-
liberately. Suddenly the room
was filled with the holding experience: that of the therapist,
that of the patient, and that of
the supervisor. That was when

the therapist told the supervisor of the patient's horrendous infantile experience of being born prematurely, just about given up for dead, and of spending two weeks in an incubator and fed through tubes. When the child was finally offered to the mother as being ready to be taken home, mother demurred—she wasn't ready. Ever since, the patient has yearned, not for paradise lost, but for paradise.

These were the experiences to be evoked and in danger of being lost if the therapist did not meet the challenge to be evocative. What was needed was the imaginative and verbal skill to make the past live, and the courage to immerse one's self in such a nightmare of deprivation in order to summon for patient and therapist (and supervisor) the sense of safety that would protect against the past horror.

AN OBSTACLE COURSE

For some twenty years, the
middle-aged patient has carried
the diagnosis of "chronic
schizophrenia." Among her
other symptoms, she also has
delusions, hallucinations, and
sometimes talks to herself while
walking out in the city. Nonetheless she had remained in
once-a-week therapy for two
years, with some diminution of
symptoms. For example, she
gave up a somatic delusion. She
did not, however, give up turning her head during the sessions
so that she never faced the
therapist, never looked in his
eyes, and did not give him the
chance to look into hers. Fol-

lowing some external losses
through illness in the family, she
increased her chronic complaints
of loneliness and frustrated
wishes to "have a relationship."
And she revealed that another
somatic symptom, which turned
out also to be delusional, had
resulted in her undergoing a
serious medical diagnostic procedure. Strikingly, she fumbled
with the name of a man with
whom she had an on again, off
again relationship, apparently
not quite remembering his
name. She also briefly imagined
that a girlfriend had intended to
kill her. (1)

(1) I suggested to the therapist
that he might consider bringing
these matters together in an interpretation. Such an intervention would include the elements
of wanting a relationship but
avoiding having one, as by not
sharing her physical concerns
with the therapist, not looking
at him, forgetting the name of
her boyfriend, and imagining an
enemy instead of recognizing a
friend. In supervision, the therapist showed that he heard and

understood the dynamics of the situation, but he said he was afraid to make such an interpretation, as he feared that this precariously adjusted patient would become unmanageably disorganized by it.

He was afraid, he said, to "push her." (2)

(2) I commended him for taking into consideration the possibility of upsetting the patient. But perhaps there were ways of conveying the information to the patient that would not be unmanageably upsetting, and might even be encouraging. One could, for instance, begin by empathizing with the patient's loneliness and need for a relationship. This would move toward establishing or vivifying what there was of a therapeutic alliance. Using that alliance one could then see the problem as something to be solved by both of them. In so doing, one could avoid the militaristic words and atmosphere of "pushing" which, after all, implies that the encounter would be one of resistance.

What needed to be evoked was an emotional recognition of the therapist's concern for the patient's predicament, and a worried recognition that if she continued to put obstacles in the path of having a relationship she would forever miss out on having one. She would create the very thing she feared: a threatening, unfriendly world. The subtle conclusion to be drawn would be that if she were able to move toward rather than away from people, she just might get the relationship she craved. And implicitly, her ally, the therapist, would help her run what she took to be a great risk.

One might, for example, say something on the order of, "Yes, you do seem to live a lonely life, and you've had some painful losses. From what you say, it seems that you yearn for more friends, men and women, whether they are romantic or social. But let's look at how hard you're making it for yourself, at the obstacles that you're putting in your path. Okay?

(Patient shakes her head in assent.) For example, you could have shared with me your thoughts and feelings and some of the worries that must have come up about your illness, but you chose to handle it yourself and not even tell me about it until it was over. (Of course it's good that you were brave enough to finally tell me today.) You work so hard at keeping your distance from your boyfriend that you partly forgot his name.

"Now why would you turn away from people even as you yearn for them? I can offer you an answer. You must be absolutely terrified at what you *imagine*—note that I'm saying you *imagine*—would happen if you allowed yourself to get together with others. If those terrifying imaginings were really true, rather than just imaginings, it would be totally understandable that you would put up obstacles between yourself and others. Yes, in fact you would be wise and ingenious to find ways of keeping your distance.

But if those imaginings are *not* true, all the worries are unnecessary and you are missing out on closeness for no good reason.

"I guess what it boils down to is whether you want to try out life with fewer obstacles, to take what you think is a great risk. I hope we can talk things over in such a way as to enjoy a feeling of safety while we consider these possibilities. You might even, sometime, see what it would be like for us to look at one another."

As to the therapist's concern about disorganizing the patient by pushing her, he was correctly following the general principle of not raising anxiety beyond the point where the patient can work with the material without becoming unstrung. The trouble is that the guideline is a general statement that has to be evaluated with reference to the unique clinical therapist–patient unit of the moment. Just as some therapists can disorganize a patient with the subtlest of unevocative or otherwise objectionable behaviors, other

therapists seldom have problems
with disorganization of this kind
because of the way they intervene. If the patient had experienced the therapist as pushing
her, she might simply have ignored what he had to say, or she
might have become disorganized through having lost (as she
would have interpreted it) an
ally, or the possibility of one.
But if the therapist had used
evocativeness adroitly, along
with other astute and supporting
devices, she could have enjoyed
the benefits of the intervention
safely.

UP THE DOWN ESCALATOR

The patient is a middle-aged
woman who has been in twice-
a-week therapy for a year.

P: I want to take some time off
from therapy—to see if I
can handle this thing on my
own. Please don't try to
convince me to stay. I'll
resent that.

T: What brings this feeling on
now?

P: I'm just going through the
motions. I'm tired, tired,
tired. I don't care about anything anymore. I'm just putting on a front with my
husband, at work, here.

Every day is a battle to get
through.

T: It's no wonder you're tired.

P: It's like walking up an escalator that's pulling me down,
down, down.

T: What are you being pulled
toward?

P: Some heavy kind of feeling.
A sadness. I don't know
why. It's with me always.
Even if I forget for a minute
and catch myself having a
good time, it returns again
and I'm sucked back into
that awful feeling.

T: You're using all of your
energy just to stay in one
place. You can't give in to the
sadness, or even allow yourself a moment of pleasure.

P: (Heavy sigh.) I feel like I
want to give up. I can't fight
with it anymore. It takes too
much energy (throws hands
into the air). Do I sound
crazy? What's happening to
me? What have I become?
I'm not myself anymore.

T: You've lost yourself in this ocean of sadness.

P: (Despairing.) It surrounds me. I'm drowning in it. It's sink or swim and I don't know how to stay afloat anymore. I'm just so exhausted. (1)

(1) The therapist chooses not to directly respond to the patient's stated intention to leave therapy. Evidently they know each other well enough so that the patient doesn't experience the therapist's silence on this subject as callous or ignoring. Instead, the therapist goes right to work in a psychological mode—"What's going on? Why now?"—and the patient then moves into a highly evocative description of her depressive experience— going up a down escalator, being sucked back into awfulness. During this she offers several openings that promise rich sources of information—putting up a good front, catching herself having a good time, assigning feelings to "it" more than to herself, and what sounds like at

least a flirtation with depersonal-
ization ("What have I become?
I'm not myself anymore").

But instead of following up
on these, the therapist adds yet
another metaphor, "lost in an
ocean of sadness." It is poetic
and probably accurately captures
something of the patient's experience. But why at this point?
The patient has taken care of the
opportunity for evocativeness.
She is emotionally open, at least
to her depressive state. What is
required now is deepening, under the guidance of psychological thinking, a psychological
processing of the intense experience implied by her anguished,
despairing comments. What are
the thoughts and feelings that
lead to wanting to stop the
therapy? Was it something in
the outer world that set her off,
or something internal?

Unlike what occurs with
many other patients, this patient
requires less in the way of the
"opening" kind of evocativeness, and more of the controlling guidance of shared
psychological thinking. Is she so

bereft that she can't think straight, or does her dramatic presentation serve other purposes? Is she, for example, trying to overcome a lapse in the therapist's concern? As a strategy one could present *her* with the problem, asking "Is it that you're so upset that you find it hard to use your usual ability for controlling feelings with thoughts?" or, "I wonder why you need for some reason to portray yourself as going up a down escalator. Could it be, even, that you think you have to portray helplessness so that I'll give up on you? Perhaps you're giving up on me. As you know, before taking action—certainly something as important as stopping our work—we need to be as clear as possible. How come, how come, how come?"

THE RELUCTANT EAGLE SCOUT

The patient is a man in his late
twenties, seen once a week for
six months, who works as a legal
paraprofessional. He begins the
session by telling of a woman
who received an "unsung hero"
award for years of doing volun-
teer work.

P: I mean that's real heroism,
    you know. She's made an
    impact and done something
    really meaningful for the
    public.

T: Not all that different from
    what you do for the public
    when you do all that pro-
    bono work.

P: I'm no hero! This is my job
and my responsibility. I'm
trained to act in a certain
way, and I just do my job.
I'm expected to adhere to a
standard of conduct, but that
doesn't make me a hero.

T: Some people seem to think
it does—like the woman
who wrote you a thank-you
letter for the work you did
on behalf of her husband,
above and beyond the call of
duty, or that kid you managed to get off drugs.

P: I'm not looking for thanks. I
just throw away those
thank-you letters. I'm just
doing my duty.

T: I wonder what makes it so
much easier for you to see
the heroism in others.

P: In my position I feel I need
to be perfect all the time—
no room for error. I can't
make mistakes. I need to be
totally pure.

T: You're not allowed to be
human?

P: I should be held to a higher
standard. I should know
better. On the job and off
the job. I should automatically know what's right and
what's wrong, without even
thinking twice about it. Like
that time I left some work
that somebody else had to
do in order to make a dead-
line. I should automatically
know better. On the job and
off the job. That was wrong,
what I did. I'll never forgive
myself for that.

T: So with years of being totally responsible, you focus
on the one weekend where
you weren't available.

P: Yeah. And look what I was
doing instead!

T: You were off having a good
time with your new wife.

P: My point exactly. I was off
having fun and they were
left in the cold. I may have
had my fun on that week-
end, but I feel so guilty
about it that I wish I hadn't
gone.

T: So the pleasure you enjoyed
was not worth it in the end.

P: I would gladly trade that
weekend for being at the
office and doing what I
should be doing.

T: You are simply human like
everybody else, but you expect yourself to act like a
saint. (1)

(1) Throughout, the therapist
tries to counter the patient's
arguments with kindly common-
sense rejoinders. Nothing much
is evoked; the patient seems to
have heard this before, whether
from others or from his own
observing self. What needs to
be evoked for examination are
the feelings that engineer the
patient's refusal to be seen as a
hero. That exclamation mark
after "I'm not a hero!" as well as
the way he threw out the con-
gratulatory letters, his bald assertion that he must be "pure," and
his diverse, reiterated disclaimers
all suggest an anxiety possibly
bordering on panic. Along with
a recognition of the patient's
disturbances, the therapist needs

to evoke a psychological curiosity about why the patient makes
things so hard for himself. What
do heroism and success mean to
him? Do they, for example, signal some kind of independence,
the logical consequence of which
would be to leave "home,"
(separation anxiety)? Or is the
anxiety engineered by a fantasy
that success would result in a
destruction of himself or others
(castration anxiety)?

The therapist's well-intended
reassurances would be appropriate should the patient be unstrung, or if he perhaps showed
evidence of shaky or borderline
ego functioning. Under those
circumstances, supportive interventions, such as appealing to
common sense and a kindly
reassuring presence would be
helpful. But if this treatment is
intended to be insight-giving,
then such an approach would
have the unhappy effect of closing rather than opening, pushing
down rather than bringing up,
playing into his need to settle for
less and dispelling any suggestion
of his being a (therapy) hero.

AT WAR WITH THE SELF

The patient has been seen once
a week for several years.

P: J. (her husband) and I fought
   all weekend and I've just
   about decided to move out.
   I cried all day yesterday and
   today, and you know I'm
   not a crier. I just have to
   move out but I don't know
   how I'm going to make it.

T: Did you decide this together?
   (1)

> (1) The patient begins to tell of
> her despair. Since she ordinarily
> does not speak so feelingfully
> and needfully ("you know I'm
> not a crier"), one would assume
> that she is in deep distress. But

instead of empathic exploration of the situation, T. shifts to a sort of problem-solving marital counseling—"Did you decide this together?"

P: He wants me to have sex. And I won't. I guess I can but I won't. I can't. I wish I could but I can't.

T: So you want to change also but feel it's impossible?

P: Yes, but I don't want to have sex.

T: I get the feeling that if you weren't married you could be left alone and not have the pressure of having to have sex.

P: That sounds good because I can't make the change J. wants.

T: You haven't always felt this way, have you?

P: No, I used to have sexual desire, energy, and hope. (2)

(2) Sometimes, of course, it is useful, if not necessary, to explore the past, and especially how the past is linked to the present.

However, one has to be careful that one does not use the past, purposefully or accidentally, to avoid the aliveness, pertinence, and intensity of the present. P.'s assertion that she *can't* make the changes that her husband requires provides a number of entries into her deeper feelings and nuances of meaning; for example, does she really mean "can't," or would a better conceptualization be that she is so conflicted about what she wants and doesn't want that she paralyzes herself? The whole "can–can't" issue indicts the roles of will and determination, the indispensable links for change between insight and behavioral changes. Her despair at not doing what her husband wants most likely encapsulates her submission, if not her masochistic need to please him. It is all moot until she comes to terms with what she wants and faces her conflicted thoughts and associated feelings.

T: What do you want?

P: He wants me to have sex with him more often.

T: Yes, but what do *you* want?

P: I want to be that way again.
(3)

(3) T. edges toward the conflict that is driving P.'s inhibition, a conflict that is telegraphed repeatedly by her difficulty not only in saying what she wants, but in seeming not to know herself what she wants. The confusion, the enormity, of her projected life change, presumably involving loss, disappointment, and rage, are all waiting to be expressed, experienced, and evoked.

T: Sounds as if you feel two different ways about this. In one way, a small part of you wants to be how you say you used to be, but a large part of you wants to just give up and go away.

P: Yes, that's it exactly.

T: I'm not sure whether you want to feel sexual or are trying not to be sexual. You sound pretty conflicted in your feelings about being sexual. Does your husband

understand this? Have you
tried to explain this to him?

P: He will never understand
this, never. He just says I
have to change. And I don't
blame him. How I feel isn't
natural. I'm wrong to feel
this way. (4)

(4) T.'s try at elucidating the
underlying conflict is on the
way to the core conflict, but
the comment could be ex-
pressed more emotionally and
with more clarity, and in less
superficial terms. Suppose T.
had said it this way: "A large
part of you yearns for the excitement and joy of a sexual life,
while another part of you fights
desperately to stay out of it. We
need to know as much as we
can about why you're at war
with yourself."

Again, asking whether she has
tried to explain her conflict to
her husband takes the attention
and focus away from her intrapsychic disturbance, where
those fantasies are that make sex
something she has to steer away
from no matter how much she

may want it, for herself as well as her husband and their marriage.

T: It's important to understand your feelings before deciding there is something wrong with them. Perhaps there's a very good reason for feeling the way you do. (5)

(5) T. wisely reaffirms neutrality, the nonjudgmental stance that helps a patient tell what is on her mind, and the need to see things from the patient's point of view.

T: Would you be surprised if I were to suggest that I think you're trying very hard not to feel anything at all?

P: Do you mean subconsciously or consciously?

T: I guess that's my question. Maybe the better answer is that you're trying not to feel at all.

P: My husband says I eat peanuts because I'm anesthetizing myself against sex.

T: Perhaps you're trying to protect yourself from pain.

P: A lot of the time I feel like a
    robot, just going through
    the motions.

T: Yes, robots don't feel hurt
    even if people leave or dis-
    appoint them. Perhaps it
    would be good to be a robot
    when necessary, free to
    choose to feel fully at other
    times.

P: Yes, yes, I wouldn't be
    trapped, a prisoner, forced.

T: As you were when you were
    raped as a child. (6)

(6) If, indeed, the rape was directly responsible for her sexual
phobia and frigidity, then the
traumatic event needs to be
evoked, as in Freud's early formulation for treatment of the
"actual neurosis." More likely,
however, the trauma has long
since been embroidered into the
whole self, damping down a life
that might otherwise soar. There
are demons here. T. and P. need
the skill and courage to look and
face them.

COLD FIRE

The patient is a young adult, a
devout Catholic, and a doctoral
student in mathematics, who is
also anorexic and self-mutilative.
She has a history of sexual abuse
by her aging and infirm father.
She has never confronted him
about this behavior.

T: When you look at yourself in
the mirror, what do you see?

P: I HATE myself. I look at
myself in the mirror and all I
want to do is cut myself
wide open.

T: Why do you think you have
that response to the person
you see in the mirror? What

did she do to deserve such
treatment? (1)

(1) "Deserve" implies some kind
of moral standard that one meets
or doesn't meet as a direct consequence of one's behavior. The
opportunity for self-exploration
in psychological terms is here
lost to a surface invocation in
moralistic terms.

"That response" is a pallid,
behavioristic, distancing way of
characterizing what this patient
reported experiencing upon
seeing herself in the mirror.
That mirror image was evidently
so powerful that the therapist
used capital letters to emphasize
it. Maybe it was more evocation
than the therapist was comfortable dealing with.

P: Nothing! But somehow she's
making herself unhappy,
and she deserves to suffer. I
mean, it's me . . . but like,
somehow . . . I can't . . .
(sigh). There's nobody else I
can be angry at.

T: There isn't?

P: (Sigh.) No one I can effectively be angry at.

T: So you blame her because
she's the nearest thing . . .
(pause) . . . and she'll
take it.

P: Damn right she'll take it.

T: And nobody else will get
hurt.

P: Right!

T: That doesn't seem fair.

P: My father always used to
say, "Life isn't fair." That's
his worldview.

T: And what's your worldview?

P: That God doesn't love me.
That's why I'm at where I
am right now. I know God
is punishing me for some-
thing. If God's supposed to
be merciful, he's not when it
comes to me.

T: So your feeling is that God
doesn't love you, but loves
others.

P: Right—God has abandoned
me, just like everybody else.
There's no reason for me to
hope, or to think I'm anything more than a piece of

shit. Why else do you think I'd want to starve myself or cut myself to pieces?

T: Perhaps you feel there is no other way to let people in on what it feels like to be you.

P: I think that I have to prove to someone that I'm really in pain.

T: The question is, how far will you have to go to prove it? And at what price?

P: I need to prove to everyone that I have a right to be angry at my father. I've always protected him at my expense.

T: You're still paying for that.

P: I *am* paying for it, big time.

T: Now when you look at yourself in the mirror and it's your own flesh you want to cut, I wonder if that's a way for you to continue protecting him from the intensity of your rage.

P: But now he's old and sick, a

helpless old man . . . it's too late. He did the best he could . . . his life was unfair too. So I have no choice but to take it all on myself, because where else is it gonna go? (Begins to cry.) My life is such a wreck. I'm so awful. There must be something fundamentally wrong with me. I want to cut myself (rolls up sleeve to reveal older and newer incisions).

T: (Observing.) You've already gone to great lengths to show me and others how you're hurting.

P: (Sobbing.) He hurt me, and I'm the one left with all the scars. (2)

(2) There are several directions one can go in this session. One is to follow the vicissitudes of aggression, chiefly her turning her anger inward in order to protect a real or fantasized other. Another possibility is secondary gain. For example, the apparent agreement between the therapist and the patient is such that the patient thinks she has to use her

dramatic symptoms to get the care that she thinks she needs and of which she is deprived.

But she tells us of the most compelling direction in her opening remark: "I HATE myself. I look at myself in the mirror and all I want to do is cut myself open." The aggression and secondary gain themes are formulations more than experiences. They could be made into experiences, cast in subjective terms unique to this patient. That would be the evocative task. But we already have her evocation to work with. She gave it to us in that opening line. She has already told us that she thinks of herself as a piece of shit. As shit, nonhuman, repellent, it makes sense to starve and cut herself. She is, in this regard, like the many murderers for whom people, even themselves, are merely things, nonhuman. She is aware, at least to some degree, of the persuasiveness of her self-hatred. She needs, however, further working through of this dominating influence, a working through that will even-

tually yield the answers to the
question of how she got and
why she maintains this sense of
self, or non-self. Her rage and
disgust need to be controlled in
words rather than acted upon.

The therapist needs to find in
himself the courage to enter
with the patient her nightmare
world. In order to be fully,
emotionally with the patient, he
needs to be aware of possible
temptations to desert the task, to
substitute other explanations
and nonpsychological disciplines. How about something
on the order of: "You may
doubt that anyone could be capable or willing to enter your
nightmare, but hear me—you
can scare you, but you can't
scare me."

STYMIED, STUMPED, STUCK

The patient is discussing a potential job change. In many
ways he has been hesitant to
move ahead in his life, to grow
up, to take on adult responsibilities. He complains to his female
therapist about the increased
responsibilities of the potential
new job and extols the virtues
of his current job.

P: The new job would involve
   more administration, coordi-
   nating things, being people's
   boss, and there could be
   budgets to do, or proposals,
   but it does sound like a good
   job, though. I don't have to
   think about it until Tuesday.

But I like taking the train to
work, like I do now. And I
hate that the new job is located in Buffalo. Buffalo
sucks. I didn't ask to be interviewed, it just happened.

T: It's not your fault that you're
going to move ahead (said
slightly teasingly and using
the phrase "move ahead"
that we've used to mean
"grown up.") (1)

(1) The therapist understands the
core conflict: the wish to grow
up is met by the fear of growing
up. The patient likely is aware
of that conflict as well, to judge
from their having mutually
settled on the deeper meaning
of "move ahead." The challenge
now is to explore the nuances of
feeling and the derivatives of the
conflict in emotionally laden
lifelike terms that escape the
deadening effects of expectable
defensive activity. That challenge
can be met to a limited extent by
a "correct" interpretation even
though it may be rendered unevocatively. It can also be met to
a limited extent by a "wrong"

intervention rendered evocatively. But for ultimate effectiveness, the challenge is met most
successfully with a correct intervention rendered evocatively.
Such interventions "go somewhere." They resonate with the
patient, so that the vibrations of
that resonance lead him into a
deeper appreciation of what he
is struggling with.

The therapist's remark about
moving ahead not being the
patient's fault is not likely to be
of much help at this point. The
intervention is framed as a reassurance, or at least could easily
be taken that way, and there are
no indications in this sample of
the therapy that the patient really needs reassurance at this
time. The remark also subsumes
the prediction that the patient is
going to "move ahead." That
can by no means be taken for
granted; the whole point of the
patient's mood and construction
of his situation is that his wanting to move ahead is met by an
equally intense fear of doing so.

The exquisiteness of his
struggle reflects how undecided

he is as to which way to turn.
The therapist may indeed be
right about her prediction that
the patient will take the path of
growing up, but the patient is
not there right now. The therapist has successfully brought him
to this climactic moment in his
intrapsychic and extrapsychic
life. It now needs to be experienced in all its inherent desperation and, propelled by that
desperation, used to understand
why he has created a paralyzing
fantasy world of fear. He needs
his struggle, with the outcome
in doubt, to be recognized.

The slight sarcasm and humor
implicit in the remark—"It's
not your fault that you're going
to move ahead"—isn't particularly helpful here either. This is
serious stuff. The patient has got
himself into a life situation that
spotlights and encapsulates an
internal rule that has governed
his life, and threatens once again
to spoil his prospects.

What the therapist is likely
striving for in her intervention is
a repetition and reinforcement
of the patient's feelings about

how he got into this conflictual
mess to begin with, and his
temptation to disavow his wish
to grow up. That probably correct reading of the situation
could have been better implemented by some such remark as,
"You sound terrified at having
allowed this evidence of your
grown-up worth to be seen;
you're probably thrilled at your
achievement, but so afraid of the
meanings and imagined consequences of your power that
you're tempted to say that you
didn't really do it. It sounds to
me as if you *imagine* terrible
things are going to happen
should you take your rightfully
won place in this world. What
we need to do is to understand
what you imagine—and I mean
imagine—will happen if you
allow yourself to be what you
can be, and fearlessly let yourself
and the world know about it."

P: I didn't ask to shave either! I
would've gone on without
shaving for years if I'd had
my way.

   He goes on briefly to
memories of that time and

then returns to musing
about the new job.

    Then he turns to how his
body hurts at the moment—
probably from too much
athletic activity over the
weekend.

P: My body hurts all over. Last
weekend I really did too
much—played softball and
tennis for several hours, two
days in a row. It's really
tough on my body.

T: Your question is, Are you
going to be okay if you
move ahead here? (2)

          (2) Once again we see that the
therapist has a good general fix
on the dynamics of her patient,
but more could be done with
that understanding. The patient
has chosen to "speak" the language of the body at this point,
which, if recognized with him,
would help their interpersonal
resonance as well as underlining
that he does use his body as a
vehicle for communication. The
questions are, "What are you
trying to say by way of your
body?" and "Why in bodily
symptoms rather than words?"

Is the key issue, as the therapist suggests, that of the patient wondering whether he will be okay if he moves ahead? Or is the patient saying more malignantly that he is *sure* to be hurt (punished), and his bodily pain right now is just a sample of what is to come if he moves ahead, a warning that reflects less an open question than a powerful conviction? The patient's implicit association from the conflict over the projected new job to the struggle against sexual development—shaving—strongly suggests that the same conflict underlies these and presumably other areas of his life. Again, he needs to be intensely aware of how his central conflict radiates throughout his life, preventing him from getting the satisfactions that he craves, albeit ambivalently.

P: I don't know. I'm just being a nut. My chin hurts, but I didn't do anything that would cause that. Each of these things is weird. Don't know what the hell is the matter with me. It's a very

regressive thing, isn't it? Like
the bunny hop, one step
backward and two forward.
Regression in the service
of the ego . . . Anna
Freud . . . no, she said,
regression in the service of
development. You could
talk now . . .

T: You're doing a lot of work
here and maybe you want to
coast.

P: Both. (3)

(3) "Regressive-progressive,
forward and backward, I need
help—from Anna Freud, from
you, somebody, anybody—I'm
caught by my wishes and fears,
my life is a battleground, I try to
escape into my body, I try to
deny my plight, laugh it off,
dismiss it as weird, it won't go
away!"—that's where the patient
is. Again, the therapist knows
where she and the patient are
in the broad outlines of their
struggle, but the therapist needs
to engage the two of them more
experientially.

   I was surprised by the semi-
accusation that the patient par-

tially wanted to coast, unless "coasting" refers to how he responds to the ever-present temptation to pull back from the assumed dangers of growing up. If so, that should be integrated into the "coast" reference. For example, one could say, "You seem tempted to shrink back from the stirrings of power implied by the new job." That kind of intervention highlights the patient's active efforts to contain his power, a better representation of what he is doing than the passive and critical "coasting."

T: We may be seeing the last stand here of your fears of moving forward—are you going to be all right, is someone going to get hurt, will your body be okay, will you lose someone you love? ("Losing someone" is a reference to his earlier worry that he might have trouble getting to his therapy hours if he has a longer commute to his new job.)

P: I know where you're getting all that, from my dreams and

stuff, but it's weird that I
would think like that. (4)

(4) The "last stand" prediction is
risky, what with the usual vicissitudes, phases, backward-and-
forward rhythm of the typical
therapy. There is always the
danger that the prediction will
be right and give rise to images
of omnipotence, or to standards
of insightfulness difficult if not
impossible for the patient regularly to reach. Or the prediction
could be wrong, and undermine
confidence in the therapist, as
well as, for some patients, indicating that the therapist is showing off.

As to the content of the prediction, that this is the end of
his fears of moving on in life,
would that it were so. Throughout this hour, he seems intensely
caught up with the ongoing,
acute struggle with his core conflict without, in his view at least,
any end (solution) in sight. The
patient is met most affectively
and effectively by the therapist's
listing of the patient's ongoing
burning questions and indeci-
sions as noted above. This de-

vice of pulling together diverse material that reflects the patient's state of mind is usually effective. The patient realizes that he is being listened to and remembered by the therapist. This contributes to the persuasiveness of the content—that mixture of confusion and clarity, hope and despair, strength and weakness listed by the therapist freezes in that moment the ingredients of their ongoing struggle and opportunity.

IN MY SOLITUDE

The patient has been in twice-
weekly psychotherapy for a year.
He is thirteen minutes late for
the session before the therapist's
two-week vacation.

P: So here's the thing. I didn't
hit traffic. I left the office
late because I was playing
several games of solitaire.

T: I wonder whether your lateness has anything to do with
our upcoming break. (1)

(1) "Separation" is more evocative than the quasi-colloquial
"break." But beyond that detail,
how does one judge the evocative potential of the therapist's

quick and bare interpretation?
On the downside is its apparent
lack of warmed-up interpersonal
context, and a seemingly flimsy
therapeutic alliance, at least in
the moment. The interpretation
also deprives the patient of doing his own psychological
thinking, thus rendering him
passive in the face of the therapist's superior ability to understand and interpret quickly. It is
also likely that the patient knew
the interpretation on the basis of
what he had heard from others
in similar situations, or from his
own previous experiences
around separations. If so, the
therapist risks being made fun
of as merely a stereotype, thus
undermining the patient's confidence in other of the therapist's
comments.

On the other hand, there
could be dramatic evocative
potential in the therapist's early
directness. If that was the strategy, it would be more evocative
to drop the "I wonder" and
milk the directness and decisiveness for all they are worth, to
say, "You chose to be late to get

back at me for going on vacation and leaving you behind. You wanted revenge."

The treatment and evocative task here is to translate the *action* of playing cards in solitary injured splendor into verbal and emotional expression. We need words to be carriers of feeling as well as meaning, words such as, "If I am going to be left alone, then I'll just be left alone and to hell with you," or "I already miss you . . . your being away frightens me" or "I feel emptiness." Such expressions, associations, and derivatives most likely were going through the patient's mind and heart as he arranged the cards in endless dull repetitions, the quiet and darkness of the empty building bordering his little circle of light.

P: I'm frustrated with this. I come in here two times a week and I don't feel I'm getting saner. Last night I watched TV instead of packing for my trip.

T: You're disappointed in yourself for not packing. (2)

(2) Once again the therapist shoots in an intervention without preparation and evidence. It is often unhelpful to so bluntly tell people how they feel. As to the content of the intervention, the patient could just as likely be disappointed not so much with himself as at his sorry lot, with which the therapist has not been particularly helpful. In other words, the patient may be more disappointed with the therapist than with himself. It would likely be helpful to evoke any thoughts and feelings the patient had during his packing for his solitary trip, especially if he compared it with what he probably imagines to be the rich life of the therapist, who is vacationing with others.

P: I wait until the last minute to pack. It's a win-win situation. I'm either a hero because I pull it off at the last possible minute, or I beat myself up—and that's good too. Maybe I'm mad at you because I'm not better yet. (3)

(3) The patient simply ignores the therapist's attempt to expand

on the disappointment theme as he goes on to detail his troubles. He barely conceals his anger, ostensibly because of his continued symptoms, but probably at their separation, as the therapist suggests.

T: What do you wish I would do?

P: Wave a magic wand. I have trouble working hard on things, and here I am working hard and it's not paying off. I sometimes feel like throwing my hands up and saying, "I'm a last-minute person. So what if I don't pack on time?" (4)

(4) The patient's disappointment becomes clearer. In addition to his disappointment about the upcoming separation, he sounds as if he is caught in a chronic sour hopelessness. He has pinned his hopes on a magic wand—The therapist? The penis? The illusion of endless constancy? Wishes coming true without his active involvement? Now he recognizes with fright and horror that the therapist

doesn't have what he needs, or at least that the therapist isn't giving it to him.

T: There would be nothing wrong with that approach, but you have trouble standing that idea.

P: I don't think I can.

T: You have real conflict here; you want to pack and you want to watch TV, and you can't do both. (5)

(5) The therapist offers a superficial reading of the patient's conflict, namely that it's between watching TV and packing. That external manifestation is more likely a symptom of underlying conflicts. One could more evocatively say something along the lines of, "I think you're telling me—and feeling—that you are pulled in all directions at once. That you are struggling with how to *be* in the world. Can you permit play? Do you have to do what others want you to do?"

P: The point is more that I don't want to work. I don't want to work but I want to be a person who wants to. I

would have been happier if I
had worked.

T: You are so unhappy with
yourself. (6)

(6) It is difficult to tell how
evocative, and of what, this last
intervention was. If said with a
genuinely convincing sense of
sympathy and empathy, it might
have established a connection
that would lower the intensity
of his complaints and help put a
humane perspective on what at
this point is mostly a litany of
complaints, accusations, and
justifications. Otherwise, the
interpretation could be felt like
another abrupt remark, banal,
condescending, or irrelevant.

P: Why aren't we done with
this? When do I get better?
I'm sick of these chronic
problems and bad habits.

T: When are you going to let
them go? It feels like they
have a hold on you.

P: That's why I should say I
choose it.

T: That is the question: Are
you choosing it or not?

P: Some part of me is, or it
wouldn't be happening. I
don't want to deal with this
anymore. I already picture
coming home to my apart-
ment, and it's a disaster. I'm
so tired.

T: Battling with yourself like
this is exhausting.

P: Maybe I should stop fighting.
Things do get done at the
last minute. My brother gets
a birthday present from me
months late. I don't like that
option.

T: But you're living it.

P: Yes, I noticed. I don't want
to do what I'm doing.

T: You know what to do, but
you don't do it.

P: I mean in terms of becoming
sane.

T: That's right. I mean, you
either have to do it one way
or the other. You can't stay
right in the middle and feel
sane.

P: I don't have a choice.

T: You really do, but you have to choose it.

P: Is that true because you say it?

T: It's reality—it's not my saying it that makes it so. But you fight against it.

P: It's not that what you're saying isn't true, but it's irrelevant. (7)

(7) This long section touches on several subjects that could easily have led to a deepening of the material, both factually and emotionally. Instead it stays pretty much on the surface, even at times becoming a bit contentious and defensive. The patient is worn out from his conscious struggles and with the way the session is going. He has not yet found relief from the feeling of disappointment in himself and the therapist, his rage at the therapist for going away, his hopelessness that he can choose to change.

T: You hope that if you can make it seem irrelevant, you won't have to do it.

P: Why are you picking on
me? This feels more like
stern advice than therapy—
what people have been telling me for decades—you
just gotta do it.

T: I think I'm responding to
your desperation about getting sane—the facts of reality are stern.

P: I just want someone to take
care of me. (8)

(8) He collapses, finally, into
the depth that he has been
avoiding—"I just want someone to take care of me."

T: That's why it must feel so
awful when I say you have to
do the thinking if you want
it, because it's the opposite
of being taken care of. (9)

(9) The "opposite of" construction is difficult to make evocative. It requires a bit of figuring
out when we would prefer an
immediate *knowing*, a "Yes, yes,
that's it!"

Perhaps the emotional strands
here could be brought together
evocatively by some such intervention as, "I get the image of

you playing a lonely game, in
solitude, pining for a nurturing
someone taking you to their
breast—hoping, hoping . . .
But instead, I go away, leaving
you with your disappointment
and defiance, your sadness and
longing—in solitude—playing
solitaire."

WHO IS AT THE CONTROLS?

The therapist of this patient
labeled as schizophrenic says,
"My first meeting with the
patient left an indelible impression upon me. By the time she
sat down in the chair across
from me, she was already im-
mobilized by terror. The terror,
which was expressed nonver-
bally, was immediately conta-
gious. My experience of terror
led me to conclude that her
ability to bind anxiety within
her body boundary was defec-
tive and self–other boundary
integrity was being eroded by
her anxiety about being alone
with me. She looked at me with
wide-eyed, speechless fright,

which I inferred was her fear
that I would kill her. After making a few introductory queries, I
found her unable to answer even
the simplest of questions other
than telling me her name. At that
moment it seemed to me that
language had little meaning to
her and in a soft baritone I simply
said to her, 'I promise you I will
not harm you. I have no intention of killing you.' At that she
calmed down: I could not tell if
the tonal quality of my words,
or the words and what they represent in language had the major
effect upon her. Slowly we began talking about what had
brought her into treatment. She
told me of a failed two-year
marriage, her failed experience
working in the post office, and
her subsequent discharge due to
mental illness." (1)

(1) The therapist raises hopes
that he is going to be an evocative therapist. He is interested in
the patient's feelings, introspects
about his own, is aware of his
vocal quality ("soft baritone"),
and is aware and thoughtful
about what in the interchange

might have been mutative. However, he risks losing the patient emotionally should his direct content interpretation be either outright wrong, or too much for her to countenance at that early moment. If she was thinking and feeling something quite different from the fear that he might kill her, then his introduction of the idea could frighten her back into her silent schizophrenic refuge. That she began to speak somewhat could have been due to having to please this person who is gratuitously denying that he considers killing her.

What she chooses to say, finally, is emotionally neutral autobiographical material, not really answering the question of what had brought her into treatment in any but the most cursory way. She could have been further inhibited by the therapist's use of the word "treatment," a distancing medical term, when the question at the moment is about her life and what in it brought them under the same roof at the same time with this remarkable opportunity to improve the quality of her life. The therapist would also be well-advised to take seriously Freud's comment about there being no "no" in the unconscious. When the therapist says he will not harm her, that he has no intention of killing her, she is liable to translate that into the positive, thus scaring herself into silence or into sticking with the bare-bones facts.

The therapist notes: "The following vignette took place about one year into once-a-week therapy. Murderous rage was present in content and in hallucination, but with me she was timid and obsequious. I accidentally introduced a new element into the therapy when I brought into the session a short, stout cup from which I drank coffee. For several weeks I drank from this cup without notice. Then one day the patient began to point and laugh wildly. I smiled and asked what she was laughing at and she pointed at my cup. I looked at my cup and asked if there was something funny about it. She laughed even louder. She said that the cup didn't fit me, and that I should have a tall cup. At the time I didn't understand this event, but over the course of several weeks, I found myself getting frustrated and angry each time she laughed at me and my cup. With some help through consultation, it became clear to me that she had now turned her anger upon me and was devaluing me through the guise of a coffee cup. When I was able to interpret this act of anger and devaluation, she became less concerned with my cup and branched out into insulting my technique." (2)

(2) The therapist is being ingenuous when he reports that he brought in and drank from a coffee cup regularly without the patient's noticing it. The patient's not commenting about it hardly constitutes proof that she didn't notice it. Perhaps she is still reverberating to what she could have perceived as his threat to kill her, that being the reason that she continues to be

in the therapist's words, "dependent and obsequious." Be that as
it may, she apparently was not
invited to offer her thoughts and
feelings about his action. If the
therapist had done so, he might
have evoked the thought and
feeling that she was being deprived while he greedily and
uncaringly nurtured himself.
Deprived of an opportunity and
encouragement to verbalize her
thoughts and feelings, she "acts"
in the form of pointing and
laughing wildly.

The therapist (with the aid of
consultation) satisfies himself
that she is devaluing him.
Maybe so. But it might have
been more helpful, and certainly
would have encouraged evocativeness, if the therapist had
asked the patient rather than
asking the consultant. The
therapist might have learned of
the possibility that the patient
was saying, symbolically, that
the therapist was a big man who
therefore ought to have a big
cup and the joke was in the in-
congruousness. He might have
gone on to learn whether this

sense of bigness was her reaction to a perceived threat to kill her, or whether it signified a sense of his competence and usefulness to her. It could be that in embracing the devaluation hypothesis without more confirmatory evidence, the therapist was perhaps doing the devaluing of himself.

On one occasion, T. reports: "I was feeling particularly insightful and cunning about a turn of events, and so I launched into an obsessive interpretation of her sadistic and aggressive wishes. After about two minutes, she stopped me with a frustrated, 'Bob! Your ego is like the Incredible Hulk!' I stopped abruptly, started laughing, and asked her what she meant. She said, 'You talk too much and it makes me feel that I'm not important.' A passionate conversation ensued around the effects of my narcissism upon her and her anger at how I was overlooking her in favor of a theory or a pet interpretation. Again, I took this as an indication that she was able to bring into the therapy an

expression of aggression, yet now
the frustration resided in her, was
bound in secondary process
word-presentations." (3)

(3) The therapist gets what he has
been asking for with his deep
content interpretations that are
given without adequate attention to the state of the patient's
defenses, the therapeutic alliance,
and the patient's feelings. As he
says, insightfully, he was driven
by a sense of being full of himself. Not surprisingly the patient
responds with frustration. That
frustration is likely driven by not
being heard. He is preoccupied
not only with himself, but with
the issue of her ability to express
aggression. He misses entirely the
expression of her feeling "not
important" and overlooked in
the face of his big-cup insight
and cunning. Yes, she may indeed have some retaliatory angry feelings, but what requires
elaboration and extension and
delineation is her feeling of being a failure (remember, she came
to treatment after failing at marriage and work).

The therapist's penchant for

laughing is dangerous to the evocative objective, as well as to the whole therapeutic process. As Freud pointed out, humor is a vehicle for carrying varied meanings, some of which are unconscious. Thus, it is difficult to know what and why anything is funny to any particular person and therefore what messages one is sending by laughing. This is particularly true with schizophrenics, who tend to extract, with exquisite sensitivity, meanings that might never occur to a better defended nonschizophrenic.

Note that the therapist doesn't agree with me about humor or the unquestioned desirability of expressing anger (see below).

T: Reports: By my laughing and owning up to my part in this interaction, I believe that I helped facilitate her ability to express her rage and anger in a productive manner. Other instances of open and outward aggression occurred in the next six months with greater frequency, and para-

doxically with less intensity
and less fear on her part. Yet
regression to primary process
communication often ac-
companied her growing ca-
pacities. For example, she
often shook her leg out of a
nervous agitation and as a
symptom of akathisia. On
occasion, I would shake my
leg right along with hers, as
much to tease her as to get a
feel for what it might be like
for her. While she normally
smiled and continued to
shake her leg, one day she
threw her leg wildly into the
air. I looked at it with aston-
ishment. Catching my attention, she did it again and
began laughing. I interpreted
this as her anger at me for
mocking her. She kicked the
air again and I said, "Oh,
now you're kicking me!"
She laughed harder. When
she was able to express her
rage and anger at me in
these nonverbal forms, I
made a great complimentary
deal of these efforts. (4)

(4) One wonders how the therapist is using "primary process communication" since the example he gives of it—the patient's shaking her leg—is unpersuasive. If true primary process accompanies her expressions of aggression, it is difficult to understand how she could be comfortable with such expressions. One doesn't regress with the expression of feeling unless the feeling is uncomfortable (or in instances of regression in the service of the ego, a high-level capability that is usually associated with creativity, or controlled wit, or sexuality). The patient's shaking of her leg, apparently unqueried, is an *action* in lieu of verbally expressing thoughts and feelings, and so a missed opportunity for evocativeness. Why the therapist shakes his leg along with her in order to "tease" her is a puzzle. It would take a very special set of circumstances to make a case for wanting to tease a patient, particularly a schizophrenic. One wonders what she is smiling at as she continues to shake

her leg. Again, we miss any indication of the therapist's trying
to learn from her what the action is in lieu of. Instead, the
therapist levels another interpretation at her about her anger,
now in the form of mocking, in
response to her sudden wild
kicking. Once again the therapist seems content with his so-
lipsistic interpretations as she
presumably is dragged along
"kicking and screaming," without being heard, without having
her inner world evoked.

Immediate deep interpretations such as those used by the
therapist throughout, but particularly in the first meeting, a
procedure once promoted by
Kleinians, used to be more in
vogue in the United States than
they are now; John Rosen
(1953) popularized that approach with psychotic patients
in his book, *Direct Analysis*. The
device can sometimes be used
for dramatic effect, evoking attention at least, but it probably
is unwise except in exceptional,
if not desperate, circumstances.
One can make a case that in this

instance it set a tone and stimulated fantasies that continued to
influence all that came afterward.
In other words the thoughts and
feelings about the therapist
could be stemming less from
figures or introjects from the
past than from real contemporary behaviors of the therapist.

Another concern about such
deep interpretations, especially
with highly disturbed patients, is
that they may encourage
thoughts and feelings that are
already too much in awareness.
Instead of stirring up what is
already so poorly managed, the
therapist should be inquiring
and clarifying and in other
ways supporting fragile ego
functions. Instead he piles on
more burdens.

As to the content of the
therapist's most-used interventions, he seems to be working
implicitly with Freud's turn-of-
the-century abreaction—catharsis
theory, as if the main therapeutic task were simply to "get" the
patient to express something, in
this instance anger. Far more
useful would be the answers to

such questions as what fantasies the patient has about expressing or not expressing anger, and what makes her angry. What, for example, are ways of dealing with anger? Does the anger stem from the past or is it in response to inflammatory behavior in the present? How does one feel when noticing a perhaps rising gorge of anger—is one frightened, or does one feel guilty, relieved, curious? The single crystallized moment when anger is expressed is far less revealing and useful than what results when the whole panoply of thoughts and feelings having to do with anger is evoked.

WINNING THE BATTLE, LOSING THE WAR

I have included the following sample of the psychotherapy of a woman labeled schizo-affective in greater detail than most of the other samples here in order to illustrate better a common way that therapists can miss evocative potential even as they seem to be doing an adequate job. You may want to read it with an eye for those moments of such missed opportunities. You may notice in yourself (as clues to the lack of color and impact in the material) boredom, irritation, puzzlement, and the beginnings of doubt in your clinical abilities.

Session #9

P: Well, I survived the holiday.

T: What happened?

The patient talked about problems with airplanes, gates, airports; her mother's driving gave her a bad back. Stopping and starting, accelerating and braking gave her whiplash. Her mother came down on her regarding her medication. She called Dr. D. to check on her appointment for yesterday. Dr. D. said it was canceled until next Thursday, December 9. She told Dr. D., on her answering machine, that she will run out of medication and she doesn't know if Dr. D. called in the prescription.

T: How do you feel about Dr. D. canceling the session?

P: Annoyed.

T: Annoyed about what?

P: Well, because I'm running out of medication.

Her mother complained about her being on medication for so

long, being a chronic mental
health patient. The patient is
disappointed about being on
medication for so long.

T: You'd like to be off.

P: Yes. (1)

(1) The implicit theme seems to
be that people—mother, Dr.
D.—are rejecting and disappointing, if not a threat to life
and limb.

The patient talked about seeing
friends who are so settled, have
families, cars, jobs, and so on.

T: You wish you had all of that.

P: Well, yes. (2)

(2) In various ways she feels
herself to be a lowly mental patient, just one instance of her
deprived and debased self. She
seethes with rage and envy at
the disparity between herself and
others. She yearns for good feelings about herself.

The patient also talked about
Leo—about missing him, how
she used to do things with him,
he'd take her shopping, and so
on.

T: He used to take care of you.

P: Yes, but now he has Irene. She's more compatible with him, she has money.

The patient complained of physical problems during her trip, affecting different parts of her body.

T: What was it like being around the people?

P: Okay—lots of pressure from them.

T: Maybe that makes your body feel worse.

P: Yeah. Like being around Natalie, cooking, and things like that.

T: You feel more comfortable around certain people and your body feels okay—body feels worse around people who make you feel anxious and put pressure on you.

P: Yes. (3)

(3) The therapist is struggling toward an interpretation about physical symptoms being the

result of unsatisfying relations with people. That interpretation would be more useful after more of her experiences of social fear and failure were evoked. She chooses physical symptoms as a substitute for feared words. Such symptoms and the caretaking reactions that they often elicit serve as a common language. She likely fears that what she might say verbally would be displeasing to others and jeopardize what little hope of acceptance she has.

The patient talked about feeling unsafe in certain neighborhoods, and recalled Leo's party. She got dressed up but didn't go because it was late and she didn't want to go into that neighborhood.

T: Who was at the party?

P: Friends of Leo's, wealthier people.

T: You were afraid they wouldn't approve of you.

P: Yes.

T: Our time is up.

P: (Getting up.) Will you be here next week?

T: Yes, I'm here every week for you.

P: Good. And we'll talk about the next couple of weeks? (Patient is referring to the upcoming holidays.)

T: Yes, we can talk about our schedule over the holidays. (4)

(4) "You were afraid that they wouldn't approve of you" is a pallid way of saying that she probably felt like they were looking down their noses at her as a scorned, despicable nothing.

Session #10

The patient is fifteen minutes late.

P: The bus was late.

T: And I received your message canceling last week.

The patient replied that she went shopping with Natalie, and she hoped the therapist wasn't angry with her for canceling. She talked about Dr. D. being angry with

her for canceling, but she gave
enough notice. She says she can
cancel once in a while. She
usually keeps all of her
appointments.

T: You hoped I wasn't angry
  with you?

P: Well, yes. (5)

(5) Again, this is an okay comment but it is lacking in color
and punch. How about, "Perhaps you were afraid that I
would be angry and feel like
getting rid of you. It seems hard
for you to feel you are safe no
matter what words you choose
to say. You probably feel like
you're always walking on egg-
shells, while in fact we are on
the same solid ground."

She talked about how she misses
Leo, he used to take her shopping. She was dating Rodney, he
wanted to stay over one night
and she didn't feel comfortable.

T: You mean sexually?

P: Yeah.

The patient talks more about
what others have and she

doesn't. She says she is in the
client role.

T: Tell me more about the
client role.

P: Being a mental health patient,
on medication, dependent
on others. I used to be on
stelazine and taking so many
pills a day.

T: What keeps you in the client
role?

The patient gives tangential,
basically avoidant answers.

T: Maybe a part of you is afraid
to be more independent.

P: Well, maybe, my Christian
subservience.

The patient talked about how to
behave over the holidays and
with friends. The therapist asked
what is holding her back from
having all the things she wants.
The patient talked about when
she went on medications and was
told she would be on them for

maybe a year, and now several years later is still on them. She talked about her diagnosis, and said that she thinks she has "affectable illness" and "schizophreniform illness and depression."

T: What do they mean to you?

P: You should know better than me.

The patient continued to talk tangentially to the end of the hour. (6)

(6) What a welter of feeling she must have about the therapist asking her about her sex life— shame, excitement, relief, terror? But all this is lost as she and he step back from the phallic brink in favor of further investigation of the client role, including medication dosage, and then finally escape into avoidance by way of being tangential.

Session #12

P: I'm late. (Takes off her coat and puts it on the floor.) Oh, look at my coat.

She goes on to talk about
clothing, her friend's clothing,
Natalie's nice clothing, and the
things she wore over the
holidays.

T: How were your holidays?

P: Oh yes—it's been a long
time since we met; they
were okay.

The patient talked about some
things she did over the holidays.

T: You said it felt like it had
been a long time.

P: Well, yes.

She offers some loose associations about friends, clothes, and
food. She tells about missing
Leo, and says that she'd called
him to get together for a drink
or something, but didn't hear
back from him.

T: How do you feel about not
hearing back from him?

P: Well, not too good.

The patient talked about Leo's
new car, and said that she "feels

castrated." The therapist asked
what she meant by "castrated."

P: Well, not having a car. It's
what men like, what they
talk about.

She talked about Leo's Nissan,
how it's a small car to drive
around, and she wished she
could drive around with him.
She also talked about other
people's belongings.

T: Sounds like you would like
to have these things too. (7)

(7) The therapist is right to
bring back the issue of their
separation, but he only skims
the surface. He overlooks the
powerful metaphorical transfer-
ential emotional meanings to
her of missing a man and interpreting his absence as part of her
castration (feelings of unlove-
ability), not having what others
have whether this be clothing,
cars, or "a penis."

P: Well, yes, but I'm not oriented like others are.

T: What do you mean by
"oriented?"

P: Like Natalie, she can stay
focused and I have trouble.

T: Why do you have trouble?

P: I don't know. I've had
trouble for years now.

T: When did things start to go
downhill?

P: At Bryn Mawr, I got confused and started hearing
voices, which led to the first
hospitalization. I had to call
a friend to ask what to do.

T: What was going on when
you felt confused and started
hearing voices?

P: (No answer, long silence.)

T: Did you hear what I said?

P: What? I'm sorry.

T: What was going on when
you felt confused and started
hearing voices.

P: Poor grades, and I missed
Warren.

T: So you were getting poor
grades and you missed
Warren?

P: Yeah, I was having trouble.
(She continued talking about
Warren.) He's married now,
with children . . .

T: So you were having some
trouble in school and you
missed him. Maybe you felt
some disappointment or felt
rejected?

P: (Silent for a bit.) Yeah.

The patient talked about starting
on stelazine, and being on it for
years.

T: So maybe it's when you
have some disappointment
or lose someone that you
start to get symptoms and
not feel well.

P: Yeah, but I don't really want
to talk about it.

She went back to missing Leo—
wishing he'd call and wondering
if she should call him.

T: What else do you think you
should do?

P: Maybe find someone else.

T: Anyone in mind?

The patient didn't answer; instead she talked about other friends, things they have.

T: You wish you had them too.

P: Yeah.

T: You know, you said earlier that you feel castrated; maybe you feel you wished you had some of the things that the others do, like nice clothing and a car and a home . . .

P: Only men aren't castrated. I'm castrated. But I'm going off . . .

T: Why do you think you go off?

P: Because I'm not oriented.

T: How can we make you more oriented?

P: Produce Leo! (Stares at therapist.) Or Warren. No, I can't have Warren . . .

T: Maybe you don't feel castrated when you have a man around.

The patient talked about the
things Leo did for her.

T: You know, I remember your
telling me about how it's hard
for you to relate to other
people, make eye contact,
because you have low self-
esteem. Maybe when you
have a boyfriend, a lover, you
feel better about yourself, it
boosts your self-esteem.

P: Well, yes.

The patient talked about a
friend who wears short midriff
dresses and tight pants, and how
this friend has a slim waist and
neat clothes and gets on the
back of a motorcycle with her
boyfriend.

T: You'd like to wear those
clothes and look sexy and
get on the back of your boyfriend's motorcycle.

P: But I don't have her waist.
(Laughed nervously, smiled
somewhat, and then fell
silent.) Are we out of time?

T: Yes, see you next week. (8)

To say that this patient feels not oriented (disoriented) can reflect either a terrifying loss of self-experience, a mild confusion, or just be shorthand for a general sense of inferiority. We need to evoke the experience that underlies her particular claim of lack of orientation, and perhaps also her humiliated imagining that others will see her difficulties.

To summarize, the patient's pattern is to circle around important issues and what is most poignantly on her mind, with only occasional dips into underlying feelings and associated thoughts. For a brief time she leaves the field entirely. The therapist tracks with her, seems to understand her, notices her defensive maneuvers, and keeps a conversational pattern going. He does all this, however, as if *following* her rather than at crucial times *leading* her. He skips along with her from subject to subject, scene to scene, event to event, skimming along the surface rather than encouraging a deeper appreciation of the im-

plications of what she is thinking and feeling, and of the
overall context in which these
details take place. The movement is circular and superficial.
The therapist would be well-
advised to latch onto the patient's occasional dips below the
surface, and explore each in
leisurely turn, involving the
patient more emotionally, as
with his help she more fully
explores her idiosyncratic world.

Some of the topics that cry
out for sustained attention are
the patient's envy of others, her
sense that she is deficient, what
she misses out on in life, her
shame at not being as good as
others, her worried anticipation
of losing others, her fear of being criticized and a touch of
defiance when she thinks she is
being criticized and threatened,
the unique ways she experiences
confusion and disorientation,
and what role she plays in her
intrapsychic world.

None of this would be new
to the therapist. What would be
new would be a way of infusing

the process and relationship with flesh and blood.

Not necessarily all at once, but one way or another, sooner or later, the patient should become familiar with herself as the following person: she feels bad about herself, as if she is not quite right, in part perhaps as a woman, but mostly just as a person. She sees others as having what she only dreams of. She at least half-heartedly tries to get what she wants but expects and finds only disappointment. She does sense that she might get what she wants, yet she is gripped with fear at the encroaching, smothering other. She runs in panic by twisting her speech and changing subjects. Instead of exploring the depths of herself for an explanation of where she is in life, she consigns the motive force to alien, outside forces such as diagnostic labels, physical symptoms, and the role of the mental patient.

To explore the meanings of her feelings, she has to be welcomed—convincingly and evocatively.

ELECTRONIC HUMANISM

I was able to get a transcript of a
tape-recorded psychoanalysis of
Mrs. C., a young woman seen
for six years, five times per
week, for a total of 1,114 sessions. I selected samples of the
analysis taken from the beginning, middle and end.

There are few records like
this around, and fewer still of
those analysts and patients brave
enough voluntarily to record
their work and make it available
to researchers. This case was
analyzed for research purposes
by other investigators.

First Year Session

The patient spends most of the
session detailing how awkward
and rejected and abandoned she
feels:

". . . somehow I wasn't anything in my own right . . . very
little interest in me . . . mother
always ignores me . . . talking
as if I weren't there. . . . I've
been rejected from the conversation . . . this image of myself
as somebody who's always going
to do stupid things and be inappropriate and have an awful
time and be afraid. Assuming I
can't dance well at all . . . only
dancing with me because he
doesn't know how to get out of
it. Where did I make a mistake?"

The patient reports a dream
about withdrawing as a way of
avoiding her usual inferiority
feelings. But the analyst, in the
dream, indicates that "you knew
what I was doing and that I'd
better stop doing it." The analyst does not take up the dream
in the form of getting associations or soliciting the dreamer's
opinion of what she might have

been trying to say or wish for.
He does go back to it toward
the end of the session this way:

"You said that, um, in the
dream I said to you, in effect,
'you know what you're doing
and stop it.' Right? What was
it?"

P: I—what you said?

T: Yeah, I mean, what was it
   that, ah, was being referred
   to? Do you recall?

P: I think I was actually sort of,
   um, gradually hunching up
   more and more and putting
   my face in my hands and
   just kind of hiding my face.

T: Ah, that's what I was referring to.

P: What feelings I was feeling
   that were making me do
   that? But it wasn't a harsh
   kind of a thing . . . it was
   almost a feeling of being
   understood . . . he cared
   and could be gentle about
   it . . . very comforting
   feeling . . . there's not any
   horrible thing happening to

me for saying it or any rejection for saying it . . . a
certain feeling of
freedom. . . . (1)

(1) The patient is working hard
throughout the session, doing
most of the talking. That isn't
unusual in an analysis of course,
but rather markedly here, although she talks, she doesn't
seem to be getting anywhere.
Much of the time her needle is
stuck in the groove of rejection
and inferiority, to such an extent
that it calls out for exploration.
Does she, for example, have the
same worry in real life with the
analyst that she has in the
dream? Is he staying and "dancing with her" only because he
can't get out of it? Perhaps there
is a clue to her suspicion in her
stark denial: "It wasn't a harsh
kind of thing." As a matter of
fact, the phraseology used by the
analyst in the dream is ambiguous on that score. It could easily
sound like a remonstration, an
impatient dictum, "You know
what you're doing and stop it!"
  Treated evocatively, this material could well have evoked in

her such images as being sadisti-
cally controlled and maltreated.
She seems to sense that she is
using defenses as a way of avoiding facing her fear of the analyst
and her retaliatory rage, both of
which she likely believes would
threaten their fragile relationship. Her references to the two
of them being nice to one another suggests a collusion not to
evoke, but to suppress frightening sadomasochistic images and
experiences.

I quoted her last comments at
some length to illustrate how
obsessionally vague she became.
It is hard to know what points
she is trying to make and the
therapist does not clarify them
either. Perhaps this vagueness is
a clue to her struggle to keep to
herself, not let it be known that
she expects rejection from the
analyst as with everyone else,
and already feels it in his silence.
The silence would be evocative,
but of distrust, frustration, and
fear rather than the experience
of a person felt to be dependable
and caring.

Later, the patient tells of her
frustration at the unresponsive,
unemotional, unevocative
analyst:

"I want your role to be something much more active than it
really is and what I understand
it should be" and "I need an
older person who knows how
to handle a conversation and
keep it going . . . I would use
my parents' friends and the
men in particular." The therapist
responds to this need and fear,
this entry into her emotional
fantasy life of older men, with
unevocative data collection:
"When was that? What year?"
    The patient tells of having
"an awfully big crush" on an
older man ". . . it sort of
scared me." (2)

(2) What a great opportunity
this would be for such questions
as "Tell me about your fear,
your thoughts about this man,
about older men, how frightened were you, what other
things did you feel, how did
you handle the fear," and so on.

Another First-Year Session

The patient left the previous
session feeling that her need for
reassurance had not been met,
and tried to get what she needed
from a friend.

T: Wanting reassurance, but
not here.

P: You mean not seeking reassurance here?

T: I mean, yeah, it's one of the
things that apparently didn't
occur to you (chuckle).
Could that be in . . . one
of the reasons it didn't come
up? (Chuckle.) That's really
what I'm getting—

P: (Interrupting.) I can't remember whether it even,
you know, did come into
my mind yesterday. It may
have, but um, you know,
sometimes I, especially when
I first come in, I find I am
here and I just have a flood
of things to say.

T: You've said that you wanted
to be able to have a place to

talk about things like that, for
example, that trouble you.

P: Now, well, I don't think I,
well, that's not true. I do
seek reassurance wherever,
even here—if I bring something up here I, I already
know that—

T: You won't get it.

P: Uh, that's not the point.
Yeah, and so even though I
would like to get it. . . .

Instead of pushing ahead with
what the patient needs "reassurance" for, what gets in the way,
why does she need it in the first
place, the analyst sounds a bit
reproachful in his reminding her
that she had previously said she
wanted to have a place to talk
about things that trouble her.
She is perhaps willing to get into
the material, but is interrupted
by the analyst. Perhaps he
thought he would feel better
about the imminent criticism by
preempting it. "That's not the
point," she says correctly, but
again her attempts are derailed.
Perhaps the patient is expressing

her irritation and frustration by, tit for tat, interrupting the analyst. Then in a flurry of verbiage she retreats from the opportunity for introspection into the surface explanation—not sure whether it even entered her mind—so that she doesn't have to talk about it in analysis. The analyst, himself in retreat from the guts of the matter, first unnecessarily reiterates the already-established fact of her expecting not to be reassured, then tries to turn the patient's anger, which he likely senses as imminently being directed to him, toward the person that the patient did choose to confide in instead of him.

What is missing is a sober, objective look at the awful situation of a patient in analysis, with its premium on speech, not telling what is on her mind, taking her speech elsewhere.

One wonders, What is missing from what should be an atmosphere of safety? Where do the patient's inferiority and self-doubt end and the analyst's responsibility to encourage the patient's trust and interest, such as that engendered by evocativeness, begin? (Incidentally, by "encourage" I do not mean active persuasion, but rather creating conditions such that the patient will not only be willing to tell all to the analyst, but be eager to do so.)

The patient then launches into several long paragraphs, uninterrupted by the analyst, in her generally typical obsessional, vague style. She suggests that the only reassurance she wants is that the analyst is listening to her, and "what it boils down to is, I'm sure you're going to (chuckle) disapprove, so I'm afraid of saying them."

Then she offers a brand-new line of thought. She ashamedly admits that:

P: I seem to have to find fault with just about everybody that I'm friendly with to some degree whether. . . . And even though in a way I might feel inferior to them, and I imagine I feel inferior to a lot of people, I still have

to find fault with them . . .
feeling very uncomfortable,
I guess, with them.

T: So your thoughts turned to
thinking about whether I
would approve or disap-
prove of things you say.

The patient then talks a bit
about her skepticism about
analysis; she was brought up to
believe it costs too much and
isn't any good. Having thus
acted upon what she said about
criticizing even her friends she
tells of discomfort at being with
the analyst as a man, has trouble
talking about "intimate" things,
". . . never made personal remarks to anybody until I knew
them for a long time." She then
tells about admiring a man's tie
and touching it to feel its texture. She is horrified at what she
did, and is sure that he was horrified also.

      She then goes into lengthy
stories revolving around money,
giving and withholding, saving
up (keeping in) and exploding,
and using and being used by

others. Then she returns to the
tie-stroking incident, the being-
with-a-man theme, by acknowledging how alert she is to the
analyst's clothes and how admiring she is of his freedom in
choosing them. (4)

(4) For long stretches her
speeches are vague, fragmented,
hard to follow. The lack of central organizing foci, the thread
of feelings and depth that pulls
things together is evident. Here
is a hint that the patient is inclined at times to retreat from
the striving, forward "phallic"
mode to a disordered, inexplicit,
ill-formed "anal" mode.

This device reaches an apogee
as a means of dealing with an
important new piece of information, as she tells of finding
fault with those with whom she
might become satisfyingly intimate. Now the piteous, self-
abnegating, anxious, and
depressed person, plagued with
inexplicable shame-laden feelings about herself, stands revealed as needing those
symptomatic experiences as a
means of dealing with a greater

symptom, the fear of intimacy. What is required now is for her to be put evocatively in touch with this underlying fear, an expansion of the "horror" she felt at realizing that she had touched the man's tie. This remains unexplored, even attended to, as the analyst says, "So your thoughts turn from thinking about whether I would approve or disapprove of things you say to what you've just been talking about."

Session 95

The patient began with long speeches about her boss who disparages her psychoanalysis, complains it takes too much time, isn't worth anything anyway, and proclaims these views in front of others. She feels marginalized by his behavior. The therapist is largely silent.

T: You feel you don't have anything worth paying attention to.

P: All right, if you want to put it that way. Or did I already

put it that way? You know,
I'm getting sick of this. Every
time we come back to the
same thing and then just
stop there. Mental block.
Done this routine many
times before. I'm thinking of
knocking all the books off
the wall again. So what
about it? (5)

(5) Parenthetically, the patient's
long speech, met with silence
on the part of the analyst, provides an opportunity for height-
ened evocativeness, here and
elsewhere through these sessions
in which the analyst is often
silent. One can observe the phenomenon in daily interactions,
perhaps especially so in groups;
the breaking of silence is of a
different order from the way it
would be if the same comment
were made in the course of a
back-and-forth dialogue. The
breaking of a silence commands
special attention, and tends to be
heard as the truth; it is persuasive.

The evocative therapist takes
advantage of the drama inherent
in the breaking of a silence. This
therapist seems unaware of that

opportunity. His silence-
breaking interventions are like as
not to be in the form of ques-
tioning some detail, or simply
offering a limp comment. The
way he breaks the silence here is
among his best: "You feel you
don't have anything worth paying attention to"—at least it has
interpretive value. But as we
shall shortly see, it would have
to be much more evocatively
phrased and delivered to overcome the patient's attitude toward its content (her wish for a
penis), and that it has apparently
already been said far too often
(and probably unevocatively) for
her to be moved, enlightened,
or persuaded by it.

From the reiteration and evident passion of her complaints
one can hardly not consider that
her expressions about her boss,
humiliation, and feeling not
understood are metaphors for
her sense of the therapist. From
the evocative point of view the
patient's dissatisfactions should
be brought into the relationship
with the therapist. Some such
remark as, "I wonder how

much of your unhappy feelings about your boss you also feel toward me right now?" would likely have done it. His content remark, referring to her feelings of inferiority based on fantasies about being a woman, merely incites her.

Not having been heard, she turns up the volume and considers moving from the agreed-upon verbal mode to action, threatening to destroy the office. She likely wonders what she has to do to be heard.

T: What about knocking all the books off there?

P: It's—I'm getting mad. I'm lying here getting mad and I'm afraid to move because I'm mad. I mean, what it seems like—and I know it's worked—but what it seems like is that you're always, no matter what I say, you're always bringing it back to this, you know—my thing about something being wrong with me. And then we just get to that, and then nothing fucking happens.

Big deal. What about it? You know, when are we going to get away from the illness and onto the cure. (Sigh.)

T: (Inaudible.) I take the idea about knocking all the books off the wall as if you wanted to knock my penis off.

P: You do?

T: Yes, I do.

P: (Laughs.)

T: That your reaction to my saying it is to want to do that.

P: Is to want to be—what?

T: Is to want to do that.

P: Well, if that's what getting mad is.

T: It wasn't just getting mad. It was also knocking all the books off the wall.

P: But why, but why are books a penis now? (Sigh.) Huh? Yeah, I think I always thought they were. That's why I read so much. I'm serious and I'm saying it

sarcastically, but I think back
about trying to be smart.

T: Yeah, I know.

P: Okay, well, I'm admitting it
ruefully, but I'm admitting it
piss-offedly. If I can't have
one, you can't have one
either. And if you won't
give me one, then you can't
have yours. But it's still the
same question. And it's still
the same feeling. (6)

(6) The patient is stirred to
bravery by her frustration. She is
exasperated by being blocked in
experience and expression. The
situation between patient and
therapist forces her further into
the castrated position that she is
struggling to escape.

None of this daunts the therapist, however, who sails right in
with the clumsy and pat transla-
tion of the patient's rage and
frustration at his unevocativeness
into the wish to castrate him.
This hastily delivered "depth"
remark about her wanting to
knock his books off, elides such
nuances as the boss standing for
the analyst's assumed power, the

authoritarianism that she complained of in her boss, and the underlining of what she takes to be her subservient position in the therapeutic relationship. All of these are, to be sure, derivatives of what most people mean by "penis envy," but the airing and examination of them in their own right in real-life terms is eluded by the way the analyst addresses them here.

So the two spar around with their mutual dissatisfactions at how this passage is going. He is unhappy that she doesn't take his favorite theme seriously enough. She is unhappy at the realization of how useless the idea is to her, and by turns is angry and resigned that the therapist must be right, or at least that she had better see it that way.

P: . . . And that you want me to be mad at you, really, and admit that I'm really mad at you. (After more of patient's complaints about the therapist revolving around envy.)

T: No, I think you're afraid that, you know, when we

started to talk about this that
you . . . what comes up is
how angry you feel.

P: Yes, at you?

T: Men. And you are frightened
that you won't be liked.

P: I never was. "When you get
to college, dear, boys will
like you," my mother said. I
don't think she said, "Boys
will like you"—that's what
I, that's what I felt it really
meant. But she said that
you will find boys that you
like, that you have more in
common with, common
interest and good healthy
things like that. Couldn't
be based on (raises voice)
fucking and sex. It had to be
a real relationship, not just
sex. Shit. (7)

(7) The therapist appears to feel
uncomfortable at the patient's
direct expressions of anger—
when the patient tries to direct
her anger specifically against
him, he fends it off by generaliz-
ing it to all men. She seems to
be evoking more in him than he
is evoking in her, other than his

inadvertent evoking of anger and frustration.

Mother says in effect, there are these two kinds of relationships, a "real" one and a false one. If one puts aside for the moment the content of her remarks, such as what the mother was trying to teach the patient about sex, one can take the patient's quoting her mother here as a metaphor for her experience of the analytic relationship: a false one instead of a real one; or, to put it another way, she yearns for a relationship of real people and genuine involvement as contrasted with the false and unevocative one of book-learning. "Shit," she says of her plight.

(After the patient acknowledges her rage—a fantasy about rising from the couch and ripping a couple of shelves of books off the wall—she ruefully acknowledges that she couldn't act on her rage.)

P: Snap up the couch like a folding bed—me in it.

T: I'm not clear about that image about the couch. I
would snap up . . .

P: No, I would. I would make it
snap up so I could disappear.

T: Snap up how? Beds (makes
snapping noise)—like that.
Snap it into a jelly roll. (8)

(8) The rage and ruefulness
could have been explored for
their emotions, but lacking that
exploration, the patient moves
to the idea, pregnant with possibilities, of disappearing within
the couch. Instead of taking up
the various possibilities in this
fantasy—she is giving up in
despair, she hates herself so
much she should disappear, the
couch as a shelter to which she
can retreat, for example—the
analyst merely and irrelevantly
inquires into the mechanics of
the activity.

P: Jelly rolls—in black blues
music, a synonym for pussy.

T: Yes I know.

P: You know a lot. Well, I just
want to tell you in case you
didn't know (Pause, sigh.)

What's a folding bed mean.
Back to the womb? (9)

(9) What the therapist "knows"
is unclear. At any rate the remark asserts his superiority—she
can't tell him anything that he
doesn't already know, and he is
sufficiently sophisticated to
know what "jelly roll" and
"pussy" refer to, all suggesting
that he is sufficiently unsophisti-
cated as to feel the need to assert
superiority and make believe
that the reference to pussy hasn't
shaken his aplomb.

She senses all this, as can be
seen in her half-sarcastic, half-
submissive, "You know a lot."
Yes, the folding bed could indeed refer to the womb. An
evocative exploration of that
idea would most likely have led
to the patient's experiencing the
"outside" world with the therapist as empty and depriving
emotionally, and that deprivation stimulated the need to retreat to a loving, cradling
relationship. Evocatively explored, that fantasy could
change her stance from a reluctant "Yes, but it doesn't help,"

to a "Yes, I do feel that way, and it hurts, and I want to understand it and make it better. Help me, I'm ready, are you?"

The patient's *cri de coeur* is evocative. She knows what she needs, though in expressing it she alternates between cowering submission and expressing herself bravely. However, the therapist has all he can manage in just dealing with what she brings.

He seems no more free at times than the patient to explore in nuance and depth, to evoke more than what is necessary for surface management (often in the guise of "depth" interpretation).

A Session Moving toward Termination

The patient begins with the sad recognition of ending the analysis coupled with the glum recognition that one of its consequences is for her to turn more to her husband. She reports a dream: "And I had a dream this morning that I . . . I was just trying to remember the different things that happened in it.

I don't know how much I can
remember . . . but it seems
almost as if it's a variation of the
dream I'd had on Monday,
where I became the man. It's
like uh, if you aren't going to
give me what I want, then I'll
take it. I hope it's just in dreams,
because that seems like it would
be a bit more manageable than if
I'm really still thinking somehow I can uh, get a penis.
      . . . the dream began when I
was a woman, and I was . . .
uh, I don't know what things
were going on. But I was a
woman for quite a while, and at
some point I think it was my
husband, but it was somebody,
you know—who was important
enough to her. So it was as if they
had some kind of permanent
relationship, whether or not
they were married, I don't know.
And uh, he was killed . . . after
it turned out that he's been
killed, I became a man . . . it
had sexual overtones. (Silence.)

T: Well, do you think that it
   might be kind of nice to be

a man and make love to a
woman?

P: (Pause.) Well, I must still
feel that way. I know I used
to. And uh, I'm more aware
of, that it can be nice to be a
woman and make love with
a man. But I must still feel
the other way, too . . .
when I want to make love,
I know I can, and I can
enjoy it enough so that it
just doesn't . . . if I want
to then it just doesn't enter
my mind now to think, well,
it must be nice to be a
man. . . . (10)

(10) Again, the therapist chooses
not to explore the dream with
the aid of associations and by
entertaining possible underlying
meanings and attending to day
residues. That would likely have
evoked clues as to the latent
content of the dream. Moreover
it most likely would have encouraged the emergence of the
meaning in more textured and
persuasive ways, rather than
starkly intellectualized ways.
Thus, the work is restricted to
manifest content.

On that basis the likely central meaning could well be that the patient fantasizes that it would help her to deal with the loss of the analyst—he is killed—if she were a man. Whatever the analyst had in mind by suggesting that it would be nice to be a man and make love to a woman, that is not where the patient is emotionally. She is concerned with how to deal with the pain of separation. Still the obedient patient, she agrees with the analyst before going on to correct him; she is more aware, she says, of thinking it would be nice to be a woman making love with a man. That, presumably, from what evidence is available, is what she has been striving for, to enjoy being a woman rather than thinking that she needed to be male (have a penis). The issue right now seems to be whether she can deal with the separation without yielding to the old fantasy that only men can deal with such adversity.

The therapist is so off-base here as to raise the question of how much the termination is adversely affecting him. Clearly, he fails to wholeheartedly pick up and react to the patient's continued working and reworking the beginning vicissitudes of grief.

T: But you think you might have, uh, sexual fantasies about Mr. X.? (11)

(11) The patient then moves more fully from the oral separation issues to the phallic one of sexuality and consequent jealousy. Now the therapist seems more comfortable, to judge from his becoming more talkative and interpretive, and probably correct in his inferences, chiefly that she is "afraid to entertain sexual fantasies . . ." However, "fantasies" is another one of those words that merely pass for communication; that is, it is used freely, certainly by jargon-prone professionals, and often enough picked up by nonprofessionals. However, if one were to ask each user to define it, one would get diverse answers from many people, and blank stares from others. "Sexual

thoughts" would have been pref-
erable. As one can see from her
comments about sexual identity,
it isn't only thoughts or fantasies
that she is terrified of, but relations, sexual and otherwise, "being with" one of those different
people—men.

P: I don't know, it depends on
how unattractive he seems
to me after I've gotten to
know him better . . . some
of these habits of his seemed
more and more annoying to
me. (12)

(12) Here we apparently have a
return of her recognition of the
device of devaluing a person as
a means of avoiding what is to
her the fearsome challenges of
intimacy.

P: I'm kind of left, well you
know, how do you relate to
a man? (13)

(13) One would, of course, hope
that by the end of an analysis she
would have more insight into
this, or at least have better control over the challenge than she
demonstrates here. She doesn't
tell us, seems unaware of, the
enormity and encompassing

quality of her fear of all intimate relationships, probably especially of those with men. That fear should have been evoked.

P: ". . . you not reacting with your own feelings . . . I can trust you, or count on you; I know . . . if I'm having fantasies about you sexually you will not take me up on it and think that's an invitation to go ahead and have an affair with me or something . . . I didn't want to happen . . . it seems like that's all I think about when I think of relating to a man.

T: Jumping into bed.

P: (Silence.)

T: I suppose that you know this is an extension of this idea that's ruled your life, that the only important thing about a man after all is his penis. So if you're going to have a relationship with him, you have to have a relationship with his penis. (14)

(14) The patient's comment about how trustful she is of the analyst can be heard as an expression of appreciation, especially so perhaps at the end of the analysis. But it can also be heard as an avoidance, a kind of excuse that removes the challenge of dealing directly with her fears of men.

What needs to be evoked in this patient, in the here and now, in the autonomic nervous system of her guts, is the dread and mixed pleasurable and painful excitement posed by the penis. Perhaps with more of that the analysis would have resulted in a better working through of that issue than appears to be the case here.

As to the use of the word, "penis," it is difficult to know from this small sample of the analytic relationship how the two have agreed to use the word, and what meanings they have at least tacitly assigned to it. Taken in its simplistic, concrete form, as in "penis envy," it is rather ridiculous. Give or take a few demands and comforts,

there is nothing that makes one
genital more or less desirable
than another. What seems to
make one or another more or
less desirable is the meaning that
people assign to it on the basis
of their fantasies, their imaginings, their associations, in short,
its symbolization. Thus, a woman
does not envy or want a penis
concretely, but rather wants
the feelings and opportunities
and other characteristics she
may associate with it. In reality
what the woman wants, as
does everybody, is to feel good
about herself, which she could
in principle feel by associating
value to the vagina. This understanding has to be clear, to this
and any other analysand, in
order to safely and sensibly use
the word at all. Otherwise the
analyst can fall into the same
phallocentric error that his
patient commits in deifying
an otherwise undistinguished
piece of flesh. Worse, such an
error severely overlooks what is
really important and cries out
for evocative treatment, namely
one's thoughts and feelings

about the overall relationship between partners that includes, but is not defined by, sexual interests and activities.

The patient goes on for several long speeches about her wanting to cry but not wanting to cry.

As we have seen, when she is troubled she is inclined to speak in fragments, to use words in ways that obfuscate. The therapist contributes to all this with only one intervention: "Why did you restrain yourself here?" (15)

(15) This patient is in obvious distress at this point. She feels tearful, senses at least that she needs to cry, yet holds herself back. One could probably cut through the obsessional verbiage and reach her heart with some such remark, which picks up bits of her struggle about crying (showing how she feels), as "You evidently expect to miss me, you even wonder how life can be without me. Perhaps it would be a great relief to feel comfortable saying that, without tears . . . or with tears, as you wish."

The patient compares her feelings about termination as akin
to that of a bird leaving the nest.
(16)

(16) This is a nice metaphor.
Perhaps it would have been
helpfully evocative to stay with
the metaphor, the bird's feelings
and thoughts, its exhilaration
and exuberance and feelings of
self-sufficiency and freedom,
perhaps along with fears of a
new way of life.

T: Well, it seems like a *good*
note to stop on today. (17)

(17) The analyst's way of closing
the session inadvertently implies
there are bad notes. That suggests, at least to the patient's
unconscious, that the analyst
makes judgments, that how she
performed, what she said and
thought and felt during the session are all up for evaluation—a
harmful evocation.

The point is not that there are
good or bad moments at which
to end, but that the agreement,
contract, and *reality* dictate how
they proceed, regardless of who
thinks what about the session.
The analyst has evoked the im-

age of himself as a judge when
he should have evoked two
people undergoing the experience of saying "good-bye."

As might be expected toward
the end of an analysis, the patient is in a reflective, surveying
mood. She begins by calling
attention to the new dress she is
wearing which leads to her
wanting and not wanting to
show herself off to the therapist,
and continues on to her feelings
of not looking as good or as
"glamorous" as other women.
She elaborates this theme of
not being as good as others, as
missing something, as having its
inception in the wish to be a
man, to make up for the missing
penis. She sees the end of the
analysis as encouraging a move
toward her husband, a relationship that has been minimized as
the result of her investment in
another man, the therapist. She
dreads leaving the analysis, the
finality of it, she says. She reports feeling "panicky" at the
possibility that she has resolved
things "falsely," that she has not
done all that she should have.

She talks of missing the therapist, and ties up his absence with her wish for father's approval and presence, which she says she had believed could only come about by her having a penis. She suggests that the relationship with the analyst could be the substitute for the missing penis. She exults a bit about what she has learned, and gives an example of handling a situation better than she would have before analysis.

This summarizes a large section of the session. The analyst made two comments. With regard to her fascination with her wedding anniversary being the same day as her last analytic session the analyst asks, "But what was the magic, then, of wanting to think that, uh, the day we separate would be your wedding day." With regard to replacing him with her husband he says, "then I'd be sort of giving away the bride."

P: And, uh, I must be thinking about that . . . having to accept I'll never have

something I wanted when I
finish here, . . . I don't
know whether it's simply that
I'll never have a penis, or
you know just that I wanted
one because I wanted my
father's approval, and I
wanted a certain relationship
with him.

The patient goes on to say that
she has gotten that missing relationship from the therapist, and
how difficult it will be when she
does not have him to turn to;
she wants him to "say some last
thing that will be with me for
the rest of my life." She recognizes that she should be able to
carry on using what she has
learned from analysis, but she is
plainly dubious that she will be
able to do so.

T: Well, uh, you know, it
   sounds like again your concern is that since you
   haven't been turned into a
   man, maybe you won't be
   able to think. But you have
   been thinking, right and left.
   You've been talking with

your husband about the
kinds of things that you used
to tell me you never talked
with him about. You con-
sider things yourself, you
understand things without
my saying anything. So
you've been doing exactly
what you're afraid you can't.
And all without a penis. (18)

(18) She does seem to be wise
and affectively involved in these
tellings. So, too, does the therapist, as he tends to be when the
penis theme is being worked
with.

Earlier in the analysis this
comment could be used to open
the way to further exploration,
such as understanding why she
presents herself as deficient even
as she demonstrates her capability. Here the analyst leaves the
statement in its gently confron-
tational and inspirational form.
The rhythm and choice of
words ("right and left") suggest
an ease on the therapist's part;
he seems to enjoy being the
focus of the fatherly, encouraging, "missing" relationship.
After some six years of working

together it may be a relief, and perhaps a helpful one, to both parties to be reminded of, and savor, what seems to be a triumph, problematical as it might be in some respects.

Last Session

P. begins briefly with direct acknowledgment "I'm feeling very sad" then launches into what seems like a metaphor about how hard it must be for Nixon to have to leave, and not get the prize that he had always hoped for. She weeps as she tells how she arranged activities to take her mind off separating.

T: What did you arrange? (19)

(19) Perhaps the analyst is none too happy either, because he here colludes with the patient by collecting data rather than joining with her emotionally. Sure enough she responds by telling of trivia of the day and family. One of her "arrangements," however, is perhaps telling metaphorically: her daughter balks at picking up her toys; that is, she doesn't want to end.

P: I guess I'm wondering, I
    don't know, it kind of
    bothers me that, you know,
    I keep feeling like crying,
    and that I feel that sad. Um,
    because, you know, I'll feel
    that sad and then I'll feel,
    but I know I'm ready. And
    so, I guess I'm thinking, well
    if I know I'm ready, then,
    you know, I don't think I
    should be feeling so sad, or
    something like that.

T: Yet, ah, you know, it's not
    pathological to feel sad at,
    uh, separating from someone
    that you've had an impor-
    tant experience with.
    (Silence.) (20)

(20) The therapist is presumably
trying to be helpful in some sort
of supportive way. However, he
does so in a notably unempathic
way. The patient didn't say that
she thought she was pathological, just that she was sad. The
use of medical jargon suggests
he is emotionally removed, and
furthermore suggests that he is
sitting there exercising clinical
judgment, and if so, what other
judgments is he silently making?

The patient hangs in gamely. She talks of loss and grief metaphorically in terms of her treasured lost grandmother. She makes a distinction between being dependent on her and missing her.

P: When I feel sadness in thinking of her, you know, there's always the knowledge that, you know, I'm capable of leading my life happily, even though I can feel sad about the fact that she's not in it. But I can't seem to get that kind of, I don't know what it is, distance, or something. (21)

(21) That could be read as an attempt to defend herself against being considered pathological (dependent).

T: Well, I'm not dead yet.

P: (Laughs, sigh, pause.) I'm also thinking about the fact that . . . there was one word you just used, that I didn't either hear, or understand. And I think it's going to bother me if I don't ask.

And you said it's not something to feel sad.

T: Pathological.

P: Oh. (Pause.) Well, I
was . . . I think this is
what I was, something has
been on my mind a lot at
night, lately . . .

She goes on to talk about her
feelings about separation. If she
feels sad, it is painful; if she
doesn't it implies she doesn't
care. (22)

(22) It is hard to tell what the
analyst is trying to achieve with
his cryptic remark about "not
being dead yet" other than to
remind the patient that they are
still working.

Perhaps the analyst wishes he
could take back his "pathological" remark. The patient, timidly,
as is her wont, hesitates, but does
at least obliquely register her
dislike of the word. This sort of
interchange provides evidence
for those therapists who are much
attuned to the need of the patient
to correct (heal) the therapist.

The patient muses about how
hard the last fifty minutes are,
and compares her impulse to a
short-circuit, like being someone seeing someone else off on
a train but who ". . . won't
wait for the train to come and
go." She then asks if he is still
recording the sessions, and without waiting for an answer suggests that her question is really
"my way of wondering if you're
going to remember me."

T: Will I have something of
you to remember you mean?

P: Um.

T: And listen to when you're
gone.

P: (Sniff, silence.) I don't
know . . . (23)

(23) The therapist correctly
senses and works with the incipient emotional issues—the
pain of separating, the dealing
with the pain by way of having
something concrete to symbol-
ize the bond and to keep the
bond alive, the patient's desire
to remain attached while being

apart, and her continued concern about whether he likes her.

P: Well, I guess maybe. I don't
know, I've wondered if
you'll miss me. And I suppose that really is all part of
that same thing . . .

The therapist's last comment of
the session and the analysis:

T: Well, the other, you know,
kind of metaphor that you
mentioned was thinking of
this as sort of fifty minutes of
waiting, uh, to see some-
body off on a train. I suppose, you know, your own
trip through life. And right
now it's time to say, "All
aboard." (24)

(24) The analyst's metaphor is
not without charm and evocative power. It is however, rather
awkward. It strains rather than
sings. Its referent—the patient's
earlier comment about seeing
someone off on a train and
avoiding the pain of the separation by not waiting for the train
to come and go—is quite different from the circumstances

where it is cited: the patient did wait the full fifty minutes. And rather than seeing someone off, *she* is leaving. Its somewhat ill-fitting quality runs the risk of depriving it of power, at best seeming rather foolish, and at worst suggesting artificiality. Still, even a mediocre metaphor, reflecting some reactivity to the emotional nuance of the moment, is better than nothing. Too often in their work, the patient has had to make do with too little evocativeness.

PSYCHOSEXUAL MODES

To be evocative one has to "speak the same language" as the other. One way of conceptualizing how this comes about is to take seriously Freud's theoretical conception of psychosexual modes embedded in drive theory (as extended by Abraham, Erikson, and others) and apply it practically. One does this by sensitizing oneself to words and other means of communication that are associated with the mode in question. I refer, first of all, to those words that are closely connected to the mode (oral: breast; anal: anus; phallic: penis), then to derivatives of increasing distance from the root biology (oral: nurturance; anal: elimination; phallic: exhibitionism and voyeurism, which are still fairly close to the bodily source), and finally to such derivatives at a still greater distance from the source (oral: ambition, caretaking; anal: hoarding, stubbornness, control; phallic: reliance on action and leadership). By correctly assessing at what level, and in what domain, the patient is functioning, one chooses the corresponding words and images that correspond to that level. That "choosing" may be conscious, rational, and deliberate, or, with the speed of what seems like uncanny lightning, one "automatically" finds oneself resonating correctly with where the patient is at the moment.

One reason for the contemporary de-emphasis on thinking in terms of drives as expressed in the psychosexual modes results from an adherence to a literal, concrete, and bounded view of what the words refer to, thus restricting oneself to words and meanings closely tied to the biological substrate. That narrowness gives rise to countless jokes that slyly make fun of such reductionism. It is no laughing matter, however, when the analyst is deaf to the patient's cues.

Let us now apply this reasoning to the analysis of Mrs. C. I am joined in this by researchers who worked in different ways with various sections of the Mrs. C. transcript. Dr. Wilma Bucci of Adelphi University employed a sophisticated computer analysis of the language used by the therapist and the patient at different times during sessions and across the full length of the analysis. Her measures included those that tapped, in particular, the dimensions of primitive-emotional to sophisticated-intellectual.

With regard to assessing psychosexual levels and themes, both Dr. Bucci and I saw the patient functioning psychosexually at levels largely different from the way the therapist saw them. In particular, we saw the patient functioning in an oral vein while the therapist focused on phallic-oedipal themes. Dr. Bucci and I saw the patient's request to have a tape recording of a session as reflecting her need for solace in the form of having something of the analyst permanently with her, not unlike a Winnicottian transitional object, and thus an oral phenomenon.

The therapist briefly seemed to share this view, but he made little of it. He seemed more invested in seeing the patient's wish for the recording as a desire to have what the therapist had, the penis, with associated envy and rage at thus being deprived. Dr. Bucci and I, on the other hand, saw, instead of a hostile impulse to rob him of his power, a metaphorical expression of the wish to share what they had produced, given birth to, as the result of analytic interchange.

How different it would be if the spirit of the analysis emanated from the wish to share the fruits of their work together, rather than the wish to castrate the therapist.

Dr. Bucci and I agreed, also, on the vagueness of the patient's speech at times, presumably as a defense against whatever was being discussed. If that defense had been worked through, the troublesome content that the patient was trying to ward off with that manner of speaking would have emerged, one would hope, in lifelike emotional terms.

Dr. Bucci and I were also in agreement that the therapist was unusually sparse in his interventions, and, crucially, we agreed in the conclusion that the therapist was largely unevocative. The result was a diminution of emotional contact with the primitive substrate, along with an increase in the use of abstraction and intellectualization.

Gill and Hoffman analyzed the Mrs. C. material from the standpoint of transference and reached similar conclusions to those made by Dr. Bucci and me, even as we ascribed our reactions to the different concepts of transference and evocativeness.

If all of us are correct about the relative lack of evocativeness in the analytic interaction recorded, then this is a classic instance of an unfortunate limitation of the therapeutic result. Neither psychoanalysis as a discipline nor drive theory can be held responsible for the result of this treatment; it is this specific administration that was lacking. What made for the mischief caused by this uncontrolled variable was the lack of attention to, and employment of, evocativeness.

One shudders to think of the many opportunities squandered through lack of attention to evocativeness. One exults at the many possibilities made available to us through exploring and exploiting, learning and practicing evocativeness.

References

Acocella, J. (1995). Cather and the Academy. *The New Yorker*, November 27, p. 56.

Alexander, F., and French, T. (1946). *Psychoanalytic Therapy: Principles and Applications*. New York: Ronald.

Appelbaum, S. A. (1966). Speaking with the second voice: evocativeness. *Journal of the American Psychoanalytic Association* 14: 462–477.

———— (1982). Challenges to traditional psychotherapy from the "new therapies." *American Psychologist* 37:H9.

———— (1990). Reflections on the use of theory in psychoanalysis. In *Tradition and Innovation in Psychoanalytic Education*, ed. M. Meisels and E. Shapiro. Mahwah, NJ: Lawrence Erlbaum.

Appelbaum, S. A., and Colson, D. B. (1968). A reexamination of the color-shading Rorschach test response and suicide attempts. *Journal of Projective Techniques and Personality Assessment* 32:160–164.

Appelbaum, S. A., and Holzman, P. S. The color-shading response and suicide. *Journal of Projective Techniques* 26:155–161.

Beaudry, F. (1991). *Journal of the American Psychoanalytic Association* 39:917–938.

Beres, D. (1957). Communication in psychoanalysis and in the creative process: a parallel. *Journal of the American Psychoanalytic Association* 5:408–423.

Bergson, H. (1979). The individual and the type. In *A Modern Book of Esthetics*, 5th ed., ed. M. Rader. New York: Holt, Rinehart & Winston.

Bollas, C. (1987). *The Shadow of the Object*. New York: Columbia University Press.

Butler, J. M., and Rice, L. N. (1963). Audience, self-actualization and drive theory. In *Concepts of Personality*, ed. J. Wepman and R. Heine. Chicago: Aldine.

Chomsky, N. (1971). *Problems of Knowledge and Freedom*. New York: International Universities Press.

Doolittle, H. (1984). *Tribute to Freud: Writing on the Wall*. New York: New Directions.

Eissler, K. (1965). *Medical Orthodoxy and the Future of Psychoanalysis*. New York: International Universities Press.

——— (1967). Psychopathology and creativity: principles and applications. *American Imago* 24 (1 and 2), Spring–Summer).

Ellman, S. (1991). *Freud's Technique Papers*. Northvale, NJ: Jason Aronson.

Faulkner, W. (1932). *Light in August*. New York: Modern Library, 1959.

Ferenczi, S. (1913). Stages in the development of the sense of reality. In *Sex in Psychoanalysis*. New York: Brunner/Mazel, 1950.

Freud, S. (1893–1895). Studies in hysteria. *Standard Edition* 11:19–135.

——— (1895). Project for a scientific psychology. *Standard Edition* 1:283–344.

——— (1897). Letter to Fliess. *Standard Edition* 1.

——— (1905). Fragment of an analysis of a case of hysteria. *Standard Edition* 7:7–22.

——— (1908). Creative writers and day dreaming. *Standard Edition* 9:141–153.

——— (1918). From the history of an infantile neurosis. *Standard Edition* 17:3–122.

———— (1926) The question of lay analysis. *Standard Edition* 20.

———— (1933). New introductory lectures on psychoanalysis. *Standard Edition* 22.

———— (1937). Analysis terminable and interminable. *Standard Edition* 23:209–253.

Fry, S. (1997). Playing Oscar. *The New Yorker*, June 16, pp. 82–83.

Gardiner, M. (1971). *The Wolf-Man by Sigmund Freud*. New York: Basic Books.

Gay, P. (1988). *Freud: A Life for Our Times*. New York: J. Dent.

Glover, E. (1955). *The Technique of Psychoanalysis*. New York: International Universities Press.

Greenson, R. (1967). *The Technique and Practice of Psychoanalysis*. New York: International Universities Press.

Hagen, U., with Frankel, H. (1973). *Respect for Acting*. New York: Macmillan.

Havens, L. (1986). *Making Contact*. Cambridge, MA: Harvard University Press.

———— (1987) *Approaches to the Mind*. Cambridge, MA: Harvard University Press.

Holland, N. (1954). Freud and H.D. (Hilda Doolittle). In *Freud as We Knew Him*, ed. M. Ruitenbeek. New York: Simon & Schuster.

Housman, A. E. (1933). *The Name and Nature of Poetry*. Cambridge, England: Cambridge University Press.

Kanzer, M. (1980). Freud's "human influence" on the Rat Man. In *Freud and His Patients*, ed. M. Kanzer and J. Glenn, pp. 232–240. New York: Jason Aronson.

Kestenberg, J. (1980). Problems regarding the termination of analysis in character neuroses. *International Journal of Psychoanalytic Psychotherapy* 45:350–357.

Killingmo, B. (1995). Affirmation in psychoanalysis. *International Journal of Psycho-Analysis* 76:503–518.

Kris, E. (1950). On preconscious mental processes. *Psychoanalytic Quarterly* 19:540–560.

———— (1952). *Psychoanalytic Explorations in Art*. New York: International Universities Press.

Lahr, J. (1999). Making Willie Loman. *The New Yorker*, January.

Mahoney, P. (1982). *Freud as a Writer*. New York: International Universities Press.

———— (1989). *On Defining Freud's Discourse*. New Haven, CT: Yale University Press.

———— (1996). *Freud's Dora*. New Haven, CT: Yale University Press.

Maisel, E. (1994). *A Life in the Arts*. New York: Tarcher/Putnam.

McKeon, R., ed. (1941). *Rhetoric*. Book III, chapter 1. In *The Basic Works of Aristotle*. New York: Random House.

Modell, A. H. (1973). Affects and psychoanalytic knowledge. *The Annals of Psychoanalysis* 1:117–124.

Oberholzer, K. (1982). *The Wolf-Man Sixty Years Later*. London: Routledge.

Rapaport, D. (1950). On the psychoanalytic theory of thinking. *International Journal of Psycho-Analysis* 31:1–10.

Read, H. (1950). *Collected Essays in Literary Criticism*. London: Faber & Faber.

Renneker, R. E. (1960). Microscopic analysis of sound tapes. *Psychiatry* 23:347–355.

Richfield, J. (1954). An analysis of the concept of insight. *Psychoanalytic Quarterly* 23:390–408.

Roazen, P. (1995). *How Freud Worked*. Northvale, NJ: Jason Aronson.

Rose, G. J. (1987). *Trauma and Mastery in Life and Art*. New Haven, CT: Yale University Press.

Rosen, J. (1953). *Direct Analysis*. New York: Grune & Stratton.

Ruitenbeek, H. (1954). *Freud as We Knew Him*. New York: Simon and Schuster.

Rushdie, S. (1999). Personal history of my unfunny valentine. *The New Yorker*, February 15.

Schaefer, R. (1959). Generative empathy in the treatment situation. *Psychoanalytic Quarterly* 28:342–373.

——— (1983). The atmosphere of safety. In *The Analytic Attitude*. New York: Basic Books.

——— (1992). Reading Freud's legacies. In *Telling Facts: History and Narration in Psychoanalysis*, ed. J. Smith, and H. Morris. Baltimore, MD: Johns Hopkins University Press.

Sharpe, E. (1950). *Collected Papers on Psychoanalysis*. London: Hogarth.

Silverberg, L. (1994). *The Sanford Meisner Approach–An Actor's Workbook*. Lyme, NH: Smith and Kraus.

Steiner, R. (1987). Some thoughts on *La Vivre Voix* (*The Alive Voice*) by Ira Fonagy. *International Journal of Psycho-Analysis* 14:265–272.

Strachey, J. (1934). The nature of the therapeutic action of psychoanalysis. *International Journal of Psycho-Analysis* 50:277–292.

Thass-Thienemann, T. (1963). Psychotherapy and linguistics. *Topic Problem Psychotherapy* 4:37–45.

Ticho, E. A. (1972). The effects of the analyst's personality on psychoanalytic treatment. In *The Psychoanalytic Forum*, vol. 4, ed. J. Lindon. New York: International Universities Press.

Trilling, L. (1955). *Freud and the Crisis of Our Culture*. Boston: Beacon.

Winnicott, D. W. (1958). The capacity to be alone. *International Journal of Psycho-Analysis* 39:416–420.

——— (1960). Ego distortion in terms of true and false self. In *The Motivational Processes and the Facilitating Environment*. London: Hogarth, 1965.

Index

ABOUT THE AUTHOR

After many years on the staff of the Menninger Clinic in Topeka, Kansas, Dr. Stephen A. Appelbaum was in the private practice of psychoanalysis, psychotherapy, and diagnostic testing in Prairie Village, Kansas, while serving as Professor at the University of Missouri-Kansas City School of Medicine. He then became the Erik H. Erikson Scholar-in-Residence at the Austen Riggs Center, Stockbridge, Massachusetts (1996–1997), after which he was Visiting Professor, Department of Psychiatry, Harvard Medical School, and faculty member of the Boston Psychoanalytic Institute and Massachusetts Institute of Psychoanalysis. Most recently he served on the faculty of the Southeast Florida Institute of Psychoanalysis and Psychotherapy, and was adjunct Professor at Southeast Nova University. The author of six books, Dr. Appelbaum was on the editorial boards of ten journals and won four awards for writing. For many years he served on the Institutional Review Board for Research and Ethics of the Regional Medical Center, Zion, Illinois.